DO NOT RESUSCITATE:

the Marvelous Beauhunks

To my BEAU-BRO DARREN - LIVE THE DREAM!

DO NOT RESUSCITATE:
the Marvelous Beauhunks

Cautionary tales from the best-looking band in the world

STEPHEN C. WRIGHT

iUniverse, Inc.
Bloomington

DO NOT RESUSCITATE: the Marvelous Beauhunks
Cautionary tales from the best-looking band in the world

iUniverse books may be ordered through booksellers or by contacting:

iUniverse
1663 Liberty Drive
Bloomington, IN 47403
www.iuniverse.com
1-800-Authors (1-800-288-4677)

ISBN: 978-1-4697-0069-4 (sc)
ISBN: 978-1-4697-0070-0 (ebk)

Printed in the United States of America

iUniverse rev. date: 01/17/2012

For Zoe

Marvelous *(adj.)*

1. Causing wonder or astonishment.
2. Miraculous; supernatural.
3. Of the highest or best kind of quality.

Beauhunk *(n.)*

1. A very handsome male.

CAST OF CHARACTERS:

Glenn Goodman—the singer

Stephen Closs—the guitar player

Adam Graham—the bass player

Stephen Wright—the drummer

Derek Supryka—the manager

(Photo—Jacob King)

FOREWORD

By Hal Harbour

Being in a band can be about hanging out, getting high and making magic, slogging hard work in rehearsals, grotty clubs with no dressing rooms, soaring emotions when your song gets played on the radio and sometimes crashing and burning. Then again, it can be about rising from the ashes and flying again.

This book could be about all of the above. It depends on where you were when it all came down.

Those were heady days at The Spirit of Radio, CFNY. I think we were all flying by the seat of our trousers. Making it up as we went along. There was no rule book to follow. The station was the only one I was ever personally interested in. Listening to CFNY was exciting. The music was always new, fresh and the voices took you to places you could only imagine.

I'd been working in a 'classic rock' environment in Halifax and feeling quite stifled. I've always been interested in scouting out new music, recordings indigenous to the local scene . . . what the kids are playing/ creating here and now . . . and I was not into toting the company line and playing the hits that came down the pike from the big labels. I'd gotten into many a scrap with program directors over the years.

Quit a few times to prove it.

I'd run out of options in Halifax, so I began pestering David Marsden into giving me a job. David was a major influence on me getting into radio in the first place . . . I'd listened to him during my Humber College Radio days when he dazzled us on the airwaves on CHUM fm. Don Berns offered me the gig . . . to write and produce his Today in Music History feature. A measly two days a week but I, of course, jumped at the chance. Packed my bags and hightailed it from Halifax to Toronto. Within a year, I was promoted to Director of Canadian Talent Development. Liz Janik was instrumental in creating this dream gig. When she left, it was a no brainer that I was it!

My job was to listen to a ton of new original music that flooded my desk everyday, go with my gut and play the best on the air. Believe me, there was a ton of it. I'd listen to a stack of tapes in my car every day on my way to and from work in my trusty Volvo wagon. Just waiting for 'the song' . . . the one!

In my role with CFNY, I was also given the green light to schedule concerts, live recordings with our Mobile Recording Unit, and host a blast of a party every year . . . the CASBY music awards.

I've had worse jobs.

It was a dream gig working with radio heroes of mine . . . Reiner Schwarz (we would go on to make music together in Funky Bummer, with Stephen Outhit). There was the infinitely creative Earl Jive and Beverly Hills, Captain Phil Evans, Alan Cross, Dani Elwell, Maie Pauts, Geets Romo, Hedley Jones, Lee Carter, Ivar Hamilton, Humble Howard and Dan Duran, Steve Anthony, John Jones, Chris Sheppard, Dave Bookman, Nicholas Picholas, Kneale Mann, Karen Fisher and the incomparable Jo Faloona (her name comes up many times in this book).

The station was full of people who loved and lived the music and the music scene. I met, interviewed and sometimes became friends with the cream of the crop of musicians and artists of the day.

I'm pretty sure I can recall the day FANTASY MERRY-GO-ROUND blasted from my office cassette player (hard to believe that cassettes were still the norm back then). Jo Faloona, a huge brit music fan, turned to me and we were both gob-smacked.

These hunky lads had captured the spirit, the sound . . . . the vibe all in a few bars. It wasn't long before we all embraced the tune and, of course, decided to give them a spot on the Modern Music CD of 1991.

They were in good company too . . . I.C.E., SKAFACE, THE COLES, PRAY FOR RAIN, DIGITAL POODLE, THE CYNIX, BEN MCPEEK, SING ALONG WITH TONTO, SATURNALIA, THE FRINGE, CHRIS BOTTOMLEY, SMALL TOWN PREACHERS, DIGIT AND SUFFER MACHINE . . . an eclectic bunch which clearly reflected the broad range of CFNY's music mix.

As I said in the liner notes:

" . . . modern, post-modern, industrial, dance pop, synth-pop, the new psychedelic, upbeat, the Bramchester sound . . . . a trip!"

Our job at CFNY was quite simple—play the music on the radio and talk it up. I was lucky because I could help pump the scene with live recordings and promo (The Streets of Ontario). But, in the end, it was down to the band. The players had to take the ball and run with it.

After the initial 'high' of airplay, the hard work began. Some kept their eyes on the prize. Some fell off the stage in a drunken stupor. Some knew the music was the thing. Some thought getting laid or posing was it. Some bands could cope. Some self-destructed. But, in the end, the music will stand for what it was and for what it is.

And the memories . . . don't get me started.

Enjoy the ride.

We all did.

EXERPT FROM EYE WEEKLY (INDIE EYE)

Thursday, February 23, 1995

SMILES, EVERYONE—Life after goofiness with Dionysian Smile

By C.J. O'Connor

Ignorance? Creeping senility? Blood pact with Beelzebub? Nope, don't rightly know what impels perfectly good 'n' alienated youth toward the accursed Happy Music (and with that new "punk" "rock" all laid out for them and everything . . . sheesh!). But that's what they did, the little reprobates: rounded up some chirpy-wirpy clap-along songs, some amusing haircuts, some bouncing beach balls for the audience and a special closing ceremony with the old magic mirror "I see Frankie! And Susie! And Joey, too!" routine (note: I may be exaggerating somewhat).

Yep, playing out the old happy-crappy over the span of three bands, namely Genetic Rhythm (ppff!), the Marvelous Beauhunks (hee hee!) and (snicker!) What Dogs Dream About (WA-HA-HAAAAAH!!!!), then finally coagulating into a supergroup which, if not seemingly sprung from the loins of Satan Himself, then at least from those of John "programmer-of-Fruvous" Jones. Dionysian Smile . . . how do you plead?

"Actually, none of us were totally happy in our old bands," admits Paul Lahey, Dionysian singer. "And yeah, we weren't completely happy with the direction they were taking. It's funny cos Steve, our guitar player [ex-Beauhunks], actually wanted his old band's name scratched off the bio in case anyone figured this was anything like the Beauhunks. It's not."

And, for reasons punk rock cannot explain, Dionysian Smile are also quite damn good, a veritable phoenix rising from a hill of shit. Sneery-snide vocals, rumbling bass and an amusingly looped cover of the only New Order song that never sent me screaming for the hills ("Love Vigilantes"), they're a sardonic, shifty-eyed look at Britpop through a warped funhouse mirror. How else to explain three-out-of-seven songs on their debut CD examining assorted sociopaths, borderline personalities and ambulatory schizoids (one titled . . . um, "Bernardo"?) . . .

Dionysian Smile play Feb. 23 at Sneaky Dee's and Feb. 25 at the Moon Room in Oshawa.

THE KRAMER VS. KRAMER TOUR —the Underdog, Peterborough

Saturday, March 7, 1992

"You guys are fucking cunts—I mean it!"

Holy shit.

Adam and I look at each other with eyebrows raised, our jaws gaping. We're stunned. In the whole time we've known him, Glenn has never spoken to anyone like that. Certainly not to us.

Moments ago, we finished playing our last song ever as a band and I'm vaguely aware of the applause that's coming from the crowd. Glenn's face is twisted into a vicious-looking snarl and I'm dumbfounded. Is he for fucking real?

As of right now I hate Steve Closs with every fiber of my being. We barely made it through the last number, *Pictures and Tears*, without punching the crap out of each other and now Glenn wants to play "mod-god" and do an encore. The last thing I want is to put on a happy face and be the nice little drummer-boy for someone else's ego trip.

I just want to get the fuck out of here. Fast.

So when Adam and I refused to keep playing, Glenn called us cunts. I'd laugh out loud if I weren't so shocked.

In the background, the punters are chanting "Wipe Out . . . ! Wipe Out . . . ! Wipe Out . . . !" and they're going mad. They want an encore. Well the punters can all go fuck themselves as far as I'm concerned.

I look at Adam and shrug my shoulders in resignation. I begin to knock out the intro to *Like Wow—Wipe Out* by the Hoodoo Gurus, and a howl of satisfaction reverberates throughout the club. Without an ounce of effort on his part, Glenn casually transforms back into his persona of good-natured geezer and sets about singing his encore.

Absolutely fucking surreal.

The Underdog has no stage so there's nothing to separate us from the beer-soaked lunatics hanging from the rafters. Those in the crowd who can still stand are pressed shoulder to shoulder, and they're dancing maniacally as Adam, Steve and I begrudgingly deliver them their stupid fucking song. Glenn smiles, sings, and slaps hands with the crowd.

This time when the song is over, and before anyone else can say a word to stop me, I tear down my kit and load my drums out the side door and into the back of my car as fast as I can. I don't say goodbye to anyone and no one says goodbye to me. Fucking assholes.

It takes nearly an hour to drive home. My girlfriend Maria and I sit in the dark and ride along in silence. She tries to say some comforting things to me but I'm really not in the mood to hear anything positive. My emotion-meter is buried in the red, charged with an alternating current of anger, humiliation, and relief. I don't know which one is the most prevalent. They're all taking turns beating me up. Except for relief. Relief is actually taking it pretty easy on me.

For the first time in over two years, I hump my drums up the stairs and into an empty corner of my flat instead of the band's rehearsal space down in the basement. I throw off my sweat-soaked T-shirt and put on a cup of tea. How the hell had things gotten so fucked up? It wasn't supposed to happen this way.

I wash the cup, crush out my cigarette, and go to bed. I fall asleep a rock 'n' roll star but when I wake up in the morning, I'm just another sad-sack, under-employed nobody.

Welcome to the working week.

ABSOLUTE BEGINNERS

Present Day

My name is Stephen Christopher Wright and I was spat out into the world on a Thursday night, back in April of 1967. The place of my birth was Oshawa, Ontario, the city that used to *Moto-Vate* Canada. Nobody asked me if this was what I wanted. Like most things in life it just happened.

For twenty-seven months, from January of 1990 to March 1992, my identity as a person became virtually indistinguishable from my position as the drummer for mod-pop icons, the Marvelous Beauhunks.

The Marvelous Beauhunks never got to be a famous band so don't bother probing your memory banks—you've never heard of us. If you have, you forgot about us a long time ago.

Back in the summer of 1991, we had a single that was climbing the charts of alternative radio station CFNY 102.1 FM called *Fantasy Merry-Go-Round.* My friends and I were just kids and we had no idea what we were doing, but for one hot summer we were touted as the "next big thing" and we were on fire.

We started out as one of the thousands of bands that were formed in garage land—fresh faces with big dreams, believing that by our own talents and a little luck, we could transform the impossible into reality.

At a time when grunge and Seattle were becoming the rage, my mates and I were grinding out the sounds of Britain from a basement in the south of Oshawa. Sharp, three-minute Britpop anthems, four years before Blur and Oasis topped the North American charts.

Fuck the long hair and flannel set; we're about Fred Perry's, soccer scarves, and all things mod.

The four of us who made up the Marvelous Beauhunks were raised on the punk rock mythology of London, circa 1977, and we desperately wanted to be an English band. We did our best to draw on the rebel poses of the Clash, the tight power-pop of the Jam, the spirit of U.K. punk, and the funky-drummer groove that made late '80s Madchester so cool.

Little did we know that within the span of two short years we'd end up hating and blaming each other for achieving exactly what we'd set out to do.

Even though my friends and I grew up in Oshawa, a depressing, grey, industrial town in Canada, you'll find an occasional—but very intentional—affectation of Brit vernacular drifting in and out of this book.

Don't like it? Then piss off. Wanker.

This is a rock and roll story.

Do not resuscitate.

The Marvelous Beauhunks at seven-eighty-two.
(Photo—Lisa Borgstadt)

PART 1
THE MARVELOUS BEAUHUNKS

HOUSE WE USED TO LIVE IN

January 1990

It's late January and it's cold. Cold outside and impossibly cold inside.

For almost three months, Adam and I have been occupying the barren top floor of seven-eighty-two, a large red brick house situated in the south end of Oshawa. Built sometime in the early 1900s, it's got great wooden doors and thick oak frames but hardly any insulation. As we've recently discovered, it's just bare plaster walls on top of brick.

The heat source for the house is an old oil furnace in the basement which possesses an unquenchable thirst for my small paycheque from the supermarket. When I'm not in classes at college—finishing my second diploma, in business of all things—the produce department of a local grocery store is where I can be found, bored senseless and counting out the hours in the back room. I'm patiently waiting for the day that I can finally tell people that I don't work in supermarkets anymore.

The single pane windows of seven-eighty-two are original to the house. When you pull back the brown, floor-length curtains, you can feel any existing warmth suddenly sucked out of the room. All that remains is your icy breath floating lazily in the air. Sometimes for fun, Adam and I will lean against one of the outside walls in his room to see how long it takes before we start to go numb. Forty-seven seconds remains the record so far.

Making it worse are the downstairs neighbours, our guitar-playing band mate, Steve and his girlfriend Damyana. They close the vents off at night in an attempt to lock any remaining heat inside their own apartment. For Adam and I, this means we sleep rough, bundled up in sweaters, socks and piles of blankets.

Our upstairs flat is decorated in a style befitting two guys in their early 20s—rock and roll. Posters of The Clash, David Bowie, and the Outlaw Josey Wales hang with pride on the walls, while a prized plaster bust of Elvis sits in his rightful kingly position on top of the refrigerator. From a Coca Cola menu board you can select one of several odd culinary dishes. For those with more dangerous appetites, "handguns and hard liquor" are available. Smiles of course are free.

Our old kitchen is bright and sunny and has a distinct '50s diner feel to it thanks to the flowered, grease-stained wallpaper, and the ever-present smell of stale nicotine and hot brewing coffee. Adam's parents donated the old Formica-topped table with matching chairs to us and this is where we meet up, smoke cigarettes, and make plans. Aside from the kitchen, we each have a bedroom and share the bathroom. There's no living room so we watch episode after episode of Kids in the Hall and the Simpsons in Adam's room on an old 1960's vintage television set, the type with walnut veneer and a broken vertical hold.

During the week, this arrangement works out fine, but it's a drag when Adam's girlfriend Lisa spends the weekends. They hole up in his bedroom with the door closed for the whole time. Whenever they're together, they project an undeserved air of superiority that I find equal parts unfathomable while completely fascinating.

As for me, I have a new girlfriend since New Year's Eve and things have been going well. Penny's her name. She's a beautiful elfin blonde with mischievous blue eyes. Needless to say, I'm smitten.

On our first movie date we doubled with Adam and Lisa. I offered to drive and we all piled into my red four-door hatchback. Near to the theatre I stopped for gas and cleaned the salt and winter grime from my windshield. As we were preparing to leave, I noticed the main exit from the gas station was lined up with people turning toward the theatre. It seemed quicker to leave from the far exit, turn onto the street that ran perpendicular, and make a quick left at the traffic signal. It was a longer way around but would be much faster than the other line-up was moving.

I put on my blinkers, checked for cars, and crossed the opposite traffic lanes in preparation for my clever left hand manoeuvre at the lights. And that's when I saw it far too late.

The concrete median.

In an instant it dawned on me. So that's why no one else was leaving from this exit. Suddenly my car was straddled across the cement divider with all four tires slowly rotating in the air.

Way to go big man.

As people drove by honking and waving, I shot Adam a seething look in the rear-view mirror, virtually daring him to say something. Anything. Without so much as a word I got out of the car and Adam took my place in the driver's seat. I didn't know what else to do so I just gripped the back bumper and pushed. Adam gave it some gas and the car slid nicely off the median, easy as pie.

To my amazement the only real damage done was to my pride, which felt as though someone had exploded a small firecracker inside my rectum.

Penny told the story like this, "You got out of the car and lifted it clean over your head with one hand and placed it back on the road. We were all in awe of your Superman-like abilities."

What can I say, my girl rocks.

THE BASEMENT (PART 1)

February 1990

Steve and I decided to form the band a little over a month ago.

We've known each other since 1985 when we met through Steve's best friend Alistair Munro. Because Ali was a bass player and I was a drummer we'd hit it off pretty quickly at college. One weekend, Ali asked me if I was interested in jamming with him and his guitar player friend.

I was duly impressed by Steve when I first met him, largely because he looked great with his thick blonde hair, Fred Perry shirt and Doctor Martens. But most importantly, I was impressed because he played a Rickenbacker 330 through a Fender Twin and came off like Paul Weller.

Unfortunately, with Steve's talent came an arrogant and passive-aggressive personality that put me off and we never got a group off the ground. That changed in 1987 when Alistair was suddenly killed in a tragic car crash. Steve and I were devastated beyond belief and we bonded over the pain of losing Ali. The only thing we could do to make sense of his death was to form a proper band in his honour.

So far it's taken us three years to get it together.

Now that Adam and I are roommates, Adam decided that he should become the bass player in our new group. But with one small hitch. He doesn't have a bass. Okay. Two hitches. He doesn't know how to play a bass, or any other musical instrument for that matter.

It seems like a worthwhile gamble though because Adam and I've known each other since Grade 11 shop class. Although he's a little moody and can take himself too seriously at times, he's got a sharp sense of humour and he's reliable. I think that Adam should be able to learn some rudimentary bass lines. If they're crap, Steve can cover it up with his stellar guitar playing.

Adam knows of a Fender Precision copy that's for sale cheap so we'll give it a try.

THE BASEMENT (PART 2)

February 1990

The first song we've learned as a trio is *Heart Full of Soul* by the Yardbirds. Steve worked out the arrangements and it was easy enough to drum to, but when Adam tried to play the root notes Steve had shown him, it sounded like crap.

Lately we've been working on *Submission* by the Sex Pistols and you can almost see Adam counting in his head . . .

1, 2, 3, 4 . . . 1, 2, 3, 4 . . .

It sounds like crap too but like less crap than *Heart Full of Soul*. I just ignore the bass and play along to Steve's guitar.

At least we're rehearsing.

THE DEMOS

February 1990

To get gigs we need a demo tape. With that in mind, we rented a four-track machine for the weekend and recorded a few songs with Steve singing. Steve's voice sounds good and since he's the guitar player and best musician in the group, it makes sense for him to be the singer too.

The songs turned out okay, but there isn't anything that makes them stand out. They sound just like standard bar-band covers, kind of flat and disappointing. There's definitely something missing.

Steve and I think the problem's the quality of the recordings.

And the bass player.

THE 782'ERS

February 1990

We haven't decided on a name for the group yet.

In the tradition of the 101'ers having been named for the address of the squat where Joe Strummer's pre-Clash band lived, we residents of seven-eighty-two are now the 782'ers.

That was my idea.

A crap name for a crap band.

PENNY (PART 1)

February 1990

After work tonight, I found a note under my wiper blades from Penny. She's had a change of heart and doesn't feel the same way about me that I feel about her. She's sorry, but it's for the best.

I sat in the driver's seat reading and re-reading that piece of lined paper. By the time I got home, my stomach was in knots and I was chain-smoking cigarette after cigarette. Before my coat hit the floor, I was on the phone to her.

I got your note. "You can't be serious? . . . Why? . . . *WHY?* . . . But what did I do?" Pleading. "Can't we work it out?" More pleading.

No.

It's my own fault. I've been way too intense. I practically worship her. No one wants to live up to that. I'd leave me too.

Thank God Adam isn't home. I don't want him to see me all busted up over a girl that I've only known for a couple of months. I might as well be wearing a dress.

Hey! I found these balls out in the driveway. They belong to you?

I know more than a couple of girls who'd enjoy being the fly on the wall tonight.

Not so cool now, eh, tough guy?

Payback is a real bitch.

CHEAT

February 1990

"I get violent when I'm fucked up / I get silent when I'm drugged up . . ."

Adam's laughing in the hallway and singing *Cheat* by the Clash. Lisa just looks concerned and embarrassed for me.

It's somewhere in the neighbourhood of two o'clock on a Saturday night or Sunday morning, depending on your perspective. I've awakened them from a sound sleep by putting my boot through the plaster wall. Seeing as I'm on a roll, I break a few more things. I'm rage personified and I look ridiculous.

The last few weeks since my breakup with Penny have been hard on me. I'm drunk again and feeling sorry for myself. I can't sleep and I look like shit. I'm a tortured, angst-ridden musician wannabe and I'm reveling in it like the pitiful, jilted protagonist in some shitty Billy Bragg song.

C'mon man. You've been through worse than this. Right? Right . . . ?

Right.

Don't forget who you are, you pathetic fucking pussy. You're a hard-rocking-cool-as-fuck-force-of-mother-fucking-nature. Women adore you . . .

I feel better for a minute. Maybe a minute and a half.

Fuck.

HONEY I WILL TELL YOU NO LIES

February 1990

The first original song that we're working up is based on a chugging guitar riff that Steve's come up with. It's a catchy cross between something punk and something rockabilly but not quite either.

I've written some dire lyrics with the title *TYNL*, which is short for *Tell You No Lies*. If you look closely enough, you'll see that my words are clearly influenced by my breakup with Penny and a Steve Jones solo album I bought back in December.

It's time to take over in the driver's seat.

ENTER GLANDMAN

March 1990

We caught a good break this weekend when Damyana's friend Cathy brought her boyfriend over to seven-eighty-two.

It turns out that Glenn Goodman might be the bastard son of James Dean and Paul Simonon from the Clash. Dressed to the rock-and-roll nines in a black leather jacket and brothel creepers, Glenn is square-jawed and handsome with a great, almost-rockabilly, quiff and sideboards. Until recently, he'd been in England playing for Leeds United FC but was cut from the team due to one too many curfew infractions.

All it took was a look exchanged between Steve and I before we had Glenn down in the basement plunking around on Adam's bass. As usual, Adam was off doing something with Lisa so he'd be none the wiser. We needn't have worried about the subterfuge though, as it didn't take us long to realize that Glenn had no more affinity for playing the bass than Adam does.

At our next rehearsal, we had Glenn come down to try singing *TYNL*. He made it through the song with a straight face and he didn't sound horrible. In front of the mike stand, he looked fantastic and that's all it took for us to be sold on him. We all went to the Ozone afterward and over a few pints we made him an offer he couldn't refuse. Glenn's now one of the 782'ers.

"UMM . . . crap name guys. We can change that, can't we?" he said.

I WON'T DANCE IN A CLUB LIKE THIS

Saturday, March 17, 1990

Is this the place to be? What am I doing here? Watching the girls go by. Spending money on beer . . .

The Tartan Tavern, Oshawa. Saturday night. Nine-forty-five p.m.

The Tartan is one of those faux Brit-style pubs found in every shitty strip mall in Canada. John Cougar Mellencamp and Bruce Springsteen are blasting on the jukebox. Jack and Diane are making out in the corner. The Boss is singing about his glory days on the high school softball team or some shit. Born in the USA? No thanks. Bored with the USA.

It's St. Paddy's Day in Oshawa. The High Holiday. Somebody please kill me.

Steve got the idea for us to come here. This isn't our usual haunt. He wants a Strongbow or two before we head to the Ozone for the night.

The Ozone is where you go if you don't fit with the mainstream. Before it was the Ozone, it was Sammy's Hideaway and before that Dudley's. It doesn't matter if you're punk or mod, skinhead or rockabilly, gay or goth. If you ride a Vespa, wear black nail-polish, like boys who like girls who like girls who like boys, then the Ozone is where you probably end up on the weekends.

Even though the Ozone is a safe haven, there's always minor scuffles happening within our microcosm. It's just human nature. The mods don't like the teddy boys. The teddy boys can't abide the mods.

That's understood. Those rules were established way back in 1979 when Quadrophenia was released, long before any of us was on the scene. And if you're a punk, you probably think that Depeche Mode is only for poofs. Not that you really care if someone's a poof or not, you just like your music harder than that.

So for the most part, it's live and let live. There's enough people on the outside that want to make our lives miserable. Now and again, every situation needs a bit of drama. So, inevitably, someone sleeps with someone else's girlfriend or boyfriend, and things start up. It's not unheard of for Glenn to be somehow involved.

That's one of the great contradictions of Oshawa. Even though the city breeds nothing but contempt for me and mine, there's always a visionary that opens a great underground club to serve as an ongoing house-party each and every weekend. I owe my entire misspent youth to these unsung heroes. On behalf of all who otherwise wouldn't be able to get drunk or laid, we salute you.

And now, thanks to a craving for cider, here we are killing time at the Tartan. Steve, Glenn and I sit at our table eyeing the other patrons with suspicion. Adam, as usual, is somewhere else with Lisa. The three of us knock back our pints and muse over potential band names.

How about . . . . *insert band name here?*

Nah. That's no good.

Well, what about . . . *insert band name here?*

Hmm, not cool enough.

The . . . *insert band name here?*

Nope, I don't see it.

Well we certainly can't stay the 782'ers. That's fucking terrible.

With Glenn in the band I figure that we can legitimately start to play off our looks a bit. We original three all have a little something to offer, but Glenn's punk-rock-movie-star looks put us in another category altogether. I'm not above capitalizing on it.

I say, "Well, what about the Beauhunks then?"

"What about the *MARVELOUS* Beauhunks!?" counters Steve.

Glenn's face opens up into a wide, shit-eating grin, "THAT'S IT—THAT'S THE ONE!!"

By the time we get to the Ozone, we have a new swagger about us. 'Scuse me. Marvelous Beauhunks comin' through. All that's left is the signing of autographs. We're unstoppable.

Coming up with a good name for the band brings us together in a way that we don't expect. We're no longer four disparate individuals trying to make our way in the world. We belong to something unique that no one else can be a part of—none of our other friends or girlfriends, just us. We may not be best friends, but we'll always be brothers.

I can't explain it any better than that.

PENNY (PART 2)

March 1990

Things happen in threes. Between Glenn joining up and our new band name revealing itself, there's just one more piece of good fortune left unaccounted for. This week, I'm laying claim to it in the form of another mysterious note that's attached itself to my wiper blades while I was at work.

Before I could even make it across the cold, fluorescent-lit parking lot, I recognized the girlish handwriting and that same lined paper from just barely a month ago. Could this actually be another note from Penny? What can she possibly want from me? Just the fact that I've been in her thoughts is enough to make me short of breath. Adrenaline shoots through me and I'm painfully aware that I smell like celery.

In her note, Penny says that she's made a mistake. She misses me and she understands if I don't want anything to do with her after what she's done. If I can see my way to forgiving her, it would be great if I'd give her a call, but she's not expecting it.

Is this a fucking joke?

After the hell I've been living through for the past month, she wants me back? After a month of looking and feeling like I've been sleeping in a gutter, she thinks she can just waltz back into my life on a whim and expect forgiveness? Does she think I have no pride or sense of dignity? I've got some fucking news for you honey . . .

. . . I know I've missed you so much too. No. Of course you were confused. It's not your fault. It's all my fault. No. I love you more. Yes, I want you back too. You're everything to me. Please don't ever hurt me again.

What can I say? I'm a romantic.

So stop being such a judgemental prick.

For at least one day in March of 1990, I can legitimately say that I have it all. My own flat, my own motor, a beautiful girlfriend that adores me, and the Marvelous Beauhunks. Young, thin and handsome. That's me.

My whole future is wide open and the options seem limitless.

I know in my gut that things are only going to get better from here on in.

PENNY (PART 3)

Friday, April 27, 1990

She did it to me again.

Of all the birthdays I'll celebrate in my lifetime, none will ever hold the same significance that my twenty-third does for me. It's always going to remain special for the single, simple fact that exactly twenty-three years after loudly bursting onto this mortal coil, Penny broke up with me for the very last time.

That's what I got for my present. Many happy returns. Fuck.

This time though, I saw it coming. Exams for college were finally finished and at long last I could relax. Penny called to say that she was coming over and I could hear that something was wrong in her voice. It's only been a matter of time anyway. After that last break-up, I knew the possibility of another was lurking just below the surface. I try not to dwell on it, but then again I'm not gonna be blindsided either. I may be dumb, but I'm not quite stupid.

My birthday is a warm, humid, t-shirt wearing day with the sun peeking through the clouds. I sit and wait for Penny on the front steps at seven-eighty-two. She parks her car on the street and sits down next to me with that look all over her face. The only thing left is to hear her say the words.

What's this? I get a kiss hello and a birthday gift. Maybe I'm wrong? Am I just paranoid?

Nope.

Ah, here it is. Things aren't working out for her. Her feelings have changed again. She needs to be on her own. Fuck me. I know how this movie ends. With me looking for a bottle of pills or some other fucking nonsense.

Not this time. I nod and take it like a man. Are you sure? You're sure that's how you feel?

It is.

Penny assures me that it isn't me, it's her. Thank you, I appreciate that. No. There's no one else. I love you. Take care of yourself. Okay. You too.

Bye.

A quick hug and that's that. I watch her drive away and I go back upstairs. I smoke some cigarettes and listen to records. The Godfathers, *More Songs About Love and Hate*. That night I go to bed early. Fuck, I feel old. A lot fucking older than my 23 years. But I'm not angry with her. That'll come later. I figure she's gonna feel the way she feels and there's nothing I can do about it. And, yes, it turns out that I am too proud to beg after all. So fuck it.

Later, I hear through the grapevine that there might be someone else after all. I don't know if it's true and I don't ask. Instead, I act like a child, put everything that she's ever given me into an oversized box and mail it back to her. A week later, there's a knock on my door and there's Penny, angry and glowering.

She shoves her own box full of stuff into my hands and tells me in no uncertain terms to "go fuck myself."

Then, she's gone.

LESS THAN ZERO

May 1990

When you throw a stone into the air as high as you can, eventually it'll stop climbing and fall back down to Earth harder and faster than when it went up. After it hits the ground, the stone will just lay there motionless. That's gravity at work and it's just schooled me like a bitch. I need something else to get me back up into the heavens again, but I don't have a single thing in place to propel me skyward. There's no launch pad, no fuel, not even a handwritten sign with an arrow that says "This End Up."

So like a stone, I just lay there paralyzed in my bed, all euphoria having long since evaporated. There's too much time on my hands with nothing to do but begin a long, slow, descent into madness. Even though I'm recently a college graduate twice over, I've given no thought as to what I'll do with my life now that I'm no longer a student. The newspapers have been saying something about an economic recession and something called "downsizing." That's none of my fucking business, I figure. I just need a job.

Although I've made a few half-hearted attempts at sending out my resume, no one's been biting. My C.V. doesn't do much to distinguish me. There's no dean's list or extracurricular activities, not even a trip to band-camp. I guess I don't show enough initiative. Anyone who does show initiative has been recruited months earlier.

Adam's already been working a respectable job for a couple of years now. He works banker's hours, Monday to Friday, and wears a shirt and tie everyday. I work at the supermarket on Mondays, Thursdays, and Saturdays and I wear an apron and name tag. I'm a loser.

Band-wise though, things are looking positive and we're starting to develop a musical identity. We've got two more original songs worked up; one called *What's All This Noise About Nothing?* that Steve wrote a few years back, and another called *Kickin' Around* that he and I came up with at his kitchen table one night. Neither is particularly great but they're serviceable.

I was hoping that as a band we'd have a harder-edged sound with more fat power chords but Steve's playing is very Pete Townshend and Paul Weller influenced. He's great at big ringing sounds and warm woven guitar lines and that's what's really been defining our sound. My style of drumming adds a powerful dynamic with lots of cymbal crashes and machine gun snare rolls. I'm the John Dillinger of drums; but only if he had epilepsy.

In order to learn enough songs to play a live set, we've raided our respective record collections. Now in addition to our three originals, we can also play the following:

My Mind Goes Round in Circles—Squire
Debbie Jones—Squire
Little Bitch—the Specials
Money—the Beatles
Gloria—Them
Heart Full of Soul—Yardbirds

COMBAT ROCK (PART 1)

Monday, June 4, 1990

Steve's friend, Matt, has offered us our first gig. We'll be opening for his band, Map of Dreams, at the Cameron House on June 4. It's only a Monday but we don't care. In fact, we're pretty excited.

For me, the idea of getting our band name in the listings of NOW Magazine makes us cooler than I ever thought we'd be.

COMBAT ROCK (PART 2)

Monday, June 4, 1990

Steve doesn't think we're ready to play the gig.

The rest of us disagree and we think he's just got a case of nerves. There are still a couple weeks for us to work through the rough patches.

We'll be ready.

COMBAT ROCK (PART 3)

Monday, June 4, 1990

The gig is cancelled.

Matt called Steve and told him that Map of Dreams is pulling out, so there's no show. Steve doesn't believe him though, and thinks we should show up anyway.

We're prepared to go to war with Matt and his band.

Beauhunk-style.

I'm not sure what that means, but it sounds badass.

Beauhunk-style . . .

COMBAT ROCK (PART 4)

Monday, June 4, 1990

We're ready for action.

It's Monday night and Map of Dreams are still listed on the bill at the Cameron House. As a result, we're headed for Toronto to launch a vigorous campaign against our sworn musical enemies.

There are eight of us spread over two cars and if anyone took the time to think things through, they'd realize that all of us are going to have to pay cover to see Matt of Dreams before we can exact our revenge. I don't think that's exactly going to "show him."

Take that Matt.

I'm also not sure what we're supposed to be doing once we get there. So far it's all been unarticulated bluster, and no one wants to speak up and ask "what exactly are we doing?" We all remain silent, hoping that someone's going to bust out some secret, last-minute strategy.

COMBAT ROCK (PART 5)

Monday, June 4, 1990

When we get to the Cameron House, Map of Dreams is already playing. It's the perfect time for us to unleash the top-secret plan.

We pay our cover charge (times eight) and stride purposefully, in a single file, to the back room where the band's on stage. We're all tightly wound and the atmosphere feels like absolutely anything could happen. My heart is racing and my breath is coming in shallow gasps. One by one, we align ourselves at the foot of the stage and we . . .

. . . do absolutely nothing.

Matt looks down at Steve from the stage with a guilty look on his face. Steve stands with his arms crossed and glares back. The rest of us stand all puffed up, trying to look tough and intimidating.

This is the secret plan?

We shuffle around and try to figure out what to do next. When Map of Dreams finish their set they come off stage to take a break. Steve and Matt go off together to have it out. The rest of us wait in silence. Whenever anyone speaks, it's in that uncomfortable, jokey way.

Damyana has the biggest balls of any of us. She walks up to the stage and detunes the guitars so Map of Dreams will have to suffer the inconvenience of retuning before they can start their next set. Even though that'll only delay them for a whole two minutes, it's more than any of us street-fighting men has done.

When Steve returns from his talk with Matt, we quietly slink out into the night without once admitting that we've failed to make any impact whatsoever. All the way home we congratulate each other on how surprised Matt was, and how cool we were in the face of danger. Matt was lucky we'd gone easy on him. It wasn't likely that he'd try another stunt like that again.

Beauhunks rule.

OK?

FABULOUS BOHUNKS (PART 1)

Saturday, August 18, 1990

We finally got a second chance at a first gig. We almost didn't take it. The Marvelous Beauhunks have decided to call it quits. Do not resuscitate.

Instead of a hip, Queen Street stage like the Cameron House, we're playing some place in Ajax called Pizza Pino's. Steve really doesn't want to play any place that might have a salad bar. I don't blame him. It's hard to make that sound cool.

In the weeks since the Map of Dreams fiasco, we've lost all the momentum we'd built up since January. We rarely practice anymore, thanks to the unreliable nature of our happy-go-lucky front man. Glenn would rather get legless with his other friends than practice the same old songs in a damp south Oshawa basement. Unofficially, we're back to being a three-piece group with no singer and a bass player who can't make the grade. I'm still in denial, but Steve's reached the end of his rope.

In less than three weeks, he's going to be a married man and Damyana's making damn sure that he's toeing the line. She doesn't think that fucking around with some go-nowhere band is a good use of his time when there's a wedding to plan.

When Glenn finally showed up to a rehearsal, Steve announced the end of the band. Glenn and Adam were pissed off but it was hard to argue for the reasons why we should continue on. Since January, we've logged exactly zero live shows and only three original songs (one of which Steve had already written two years ago). It's time to move on.

The only reason we're even playing this one gig is that it was handed to us by a guy named Dan, who I work with at the supermarket. Dan plays guitar in a band called M.I.U. and they're also playing their last show. He knows that I've got a group, so he asked me if we wanted to open for them at Pizza Pino's on the eighteenth. I told him sure thing and asked who *Pete Zapino* was.

At any rate, despite Steve's reluctance to drag things out, we've decided to go out with a bang instead of a whimper.

What have we got to lose?

FABULOUS BOHUNKS (PART 2)

Sunday, August 19, 1990

Our show at Pizza Pino's kicked ass last night.

No one was more surprised than we were.

We loaded in around 6:30 and the first thing we saw was a handbill advertising the show, taped to the door. As the headliners, M.I.U. was listed with the biggest lettering. But what was underneath in slightly smaller font, made me laugh out loud. Complete with long coarse hairs and stink lines around the text, was "The Fabulous Bohunks." I can see where Marvelous and Fabulous may seem interchangeable but "Bohunks" is a derogatory slur that I learned about from my Ukrainian grandfather.

I guess I failed to make that connection when we named the band.

To Steve's relief, there was no salad bar in sight. Instead there was a small stage with lights and a PA set up in the back corner. After the backline was in place, we retired to our dressing room which fortunately doubled as the men's room. With the realization that we were finally about to play rock and roll in front of a live audience, a knot of fear made its way into my bladder and stayed there until it was time to take the stage.

We played 10 songs and received generous applause from the 40, or so, kids in the crowd. Heads were bopping along and no one laughed at us when we were done. We'd made it through, and sold ourselves as a real band.

Afterwards, people wanted to know who we were, how long we'd been playing together, and when the next show was.

We felt like stars.

FOUR FUNERALS AND A WEDDING

Saturday, August 25, 1990

"Please get down from there—you're embarrassing me . . ."

Damyana's sobbing from the foot of the stage. Mascara's running down her cheeks.

"Fuck off—I'll do what I want . . ." slurs Steve into the microphone as he lurches drunkenly, borrowed guitar in hand.

"*1, 2, 3, 4 . . . Burnin', lootin', rapin' and-a-shootin'* . . ." sings the brand-new bridegroom while a line-up of family, friends, and well-wishers makes a run for the exits. The head-table itself might as well be on fire. Damyana hasn't even thrown her bouquet.

I sit there mortified behind the drums. All the gear we're using belongs to the polka band that's been hired to play Steve and Damyana's wedding reception. We're gonna be in such deep shit when this is over.

After a lengthy-feedback-drenched guitar solo; Steve takes a moment to tune-up and fiddle with the guitar-player's amp. Ping-ping . . . crunch. Ping-ping . . . Cr-unch. Ping-ping . . . CR-UN-CH! His new father-in-law seizes the opportunity to escort Steve from the stage when all of a sudden, in one fluid movement, Steve has him in a headlock and shouts at him, "Fuck off, pal!"

Just 20 minutes prior, all had been calm and everyone had been having a nice time dancing to the polka band or mingling about. I was in the parking lot taking a romantic stroll with Glenn's girlfriend when all of a sudden, over the loudspeaker, was a request for "the Marvelous Beauhunks to report to the stage . . ." Sorry doll, duty calls. I ditched Cathy thinking that I might pick things up where I left off, a little later on.

The leader of the polka band addressed the crowd, "Since the groom plays guitar in his own band, we're going to take a little break and the Marvelous Beauhunks are going to perform a few songs for you." Some polite applause echoed in the hall.

Because of our unexpectedly positive reaction at Pizza Pino's the week before; we're arrogant and cocky and we can't wait for another chance to show our stuff. Glenn's been eyeing the cute girl in the red dress so he's anxious to have a go. We start with *TYNL*. What's this? I can't hear a goddamn thing. No bass, no guitar, no vocal. Just drums. Fuck . . . there's no stage monitors. I start to panic.

Next is *Debbie Jones*. We start and stop and start and stop again. It takes three attempts before we finally all come in at the right time. Adam keeps looking at me for the cues, but I'm lost. The song goes on for 10 minutes because we don't know where to end it. Then, thanks to the six ounces of scotch he'd consumed immediately before taking stage, Steve transformed with a red-eyed fury into "*that*" guy. The mean-looking one with the sobbing bride and the new father-in-law in a headlock. Things continue to deteriorate.

Damyana's dad manages to slip out of Steve's grip and he gets himself to a safe distance. Poor Damyana lights into Steve as he stumbles around, managing to step on her dress and tearing the fabric in the process. There's no possible way that he's going to keep his stomach contents from reintroducing themselves to the outside world, so Glenn hustles him off into the trees and then to the back seat of his car. Steve barfs his brains out while Damyana runs around going berserk. The hall is practically empty now.

"Fuck me. Thank God that's over." I think with a mind to planning my own escape.

Looking up, I'm accosted by a pissed-off polka-drummer who's holding out a bent and cracked splash cymbal. Did I do that? His band mates are standing closely behind him. They aren't too happy either. The painful exchange of $150 helps to extinguish some of their murderous intent. I suppose I really don't need to eat for the next month. Fuck. I've never even seen a splash cymbal before. I didn't know that you aren't supposed to hit them hard like a regular cymbal. I'm a fucking punk rock drummer. What do I know from splash cymbals?

It's time to go home. Feets don't fail me now.

Back at seven-eighty-two, Steve spends his wedding night passed out on the couch while his mother helps Damyana out of her dress. I creep up the stairs as quietly as I can. There's no way I'm going to face Damyana. In only four more hours, they're due for a flight to Yugoslavia for a honeymoon and I'll be safe from her wrath. I'm convinced that there's no more band after this. Fuck. Steve will be lucky to be alive, let alone still married.

For the next three weeks I have a sick feeling in the pit of my stomach, waiting for them to return and for the hammer to drop. Better to have taken my lumps up front, I think. Adam seems strangely unaffected by his part in the whole debacle and for him it's business as usual.

So goes the illustrious second performance of the Marvelous Beauhunks.

CITY ASLEEP

September 1990

Steve and Damyana came back from Yugoslavia still married and in good spirits. Yes, there's still a band. To my amazement, the "wedding incident" hasn't been brought up. I'm relieved on many levels.

We've resumed rehearsals with a new lease on life and there's energy and excitement in the air. After our small taste of live performance, we know we've got the goods but now we need to book gigs. We've discussed it ad nauseum and we all agree that a press-kit and a proper demo-tape, from a proper studio is needed. Adam's girlfriend is a hobby photographer so, on Sunday, September 23rd, Lisa captures the essence of the Marvelous Beauhunks in black and white with her 35mm camera.

Attempting to look cool, we strike rock star poses in the basement and various locations outside seven-eighty-two. Glenn has his rockabilly look and Adam's dressed in his biker jacket and plain tee-shirt. Steve's wearing a jean jacket and Doctor Martens, while I appear rough and ready in my pea coat and three day's beard stubble. After shooting several rolls of film, Lisa's tired of our vanity and she's rolling her eyes. Adam says goodbye and they excuse themselves for the day.

Steve, Glenn, and I decide to give the basement a much needed makeover. Up until now, our practice space has been a dirty and not particularly nice place to spend time. We sweep it out, lay down some carpeting and install a borrowed dehumidifier. An old couch is brought downstairs and some Madness and Jam posters are pinned up. In one fell swoop our cold, damp echo chamber has been transformed into a bright comfortable sanctuary.

That evening, the three of us sit in our new basement with some beer and we make plans for the future. The days have been getting shorter and the autumn air has been getting crisp at night. It's so comfortable sitting on that old couch that I can almost forget that tomorrow means another early morning at the supermarket. Instead of my usual attitude of cynicism, I'm full of hope and confidence. Tonight, it's good to be in the Marvelous Beauhunks; at least for some of us.

Because Adam generally keeps himself apart from the camaraderie within the band, he makes it difficult for Steve to overlook his shortcomings as a bass player. Now, the next six months will be especially tough on him as Lisa has taken a contract to work in Edmonton. This will mark the longest period that they've been apart in the last three years.

Adam surprised us when his impending separation from Lisa inspired him to put pen to paper and he came up with the lyrics to a song called *City Asleep*. Steve matched Adam's lyrics against a Stone Roses inspired guitar riff and the basis for the next Marvelous Beauhunks original was born.

Every cloud has a silver lining.

And with that, we're on our way.

Stephen Wright at seven-eighty-two
(Photo—Lisa Borgstadt)

ROUND AND AROUND AND AROUND

October 1990

October has been a prolific period for us creatively. In addition to *City Asleep*, we've worked up two more original songs.

The first is a moody song in the key of D-minor, entitled *Dare to Dream*. Steve's playing on this number pays tribute to the Turtles' *Happy Together* in the shape of an intricate guitar solo at the end of the song. Lyrically, it's just another recount of my typical subject matter, namely girls, break-ups and loneliness. Some more hokey, grade-school poetry set to music.

Dare to dream that the world's gone crazy
When the girl you love won't look away
And there's nothing left to make it easy
But the routine of a routine day . . .

The second number is called *Fantasy Merry-Go-Round*. This one originates from a set of lyrics that Glenn wrote. I like the title, but I'm not overly impressed with the subject matter of his song, particularly the line, "Is this a fantasy or just a wet dream?" I tell Glenn that I'm going to write my own version and he doesn't mind.

To get myself in the mood, I sit down at the table under the yellow light of our old swag lamp and stare past the red curtains, out the kitchen window. The weather is characteristic of late October and the sun is a faded orange ball that hangs low in the four o'clock sky. Fallen leaves are being swept around by small gusts of wind. These are the conditions that make it easy for me to get inside my own head and write down whatever comes out. All I need to do is make myself feel bad and the self-pity starts to flow.

Conveniently lost while she's caught in her cause
So deep in cloud cover—habitual sunrise
She's found her conscience has nowhere to turn
In time realizing she can't carry on
She's trapped on a fantasy merry-go-round . . .

More melodramatic horseshit . . . .

What makes me laugh is the music that Steve chooses to accompany my introspective and heart heavy words. He picks the bounciest 1960s' beach-party riff he can think of and plays it in a bright, sunny, major key. I don't know if that's his intention, but he couldn't have come up with a more obvious contrast if he'd tried.

When we worked up the arrangement for *Fantasy Merry-Go-Round*, I decided that I should start us off with a one bar, 16-beat snare roll. During one go around, I was taking the piss and kept the snare roll ringing for two bars instead of one. I didn't expect anyone to take me seriously but Steve, Glenn, and Adam unanimously agreed that this is the way to start off the song.

From now on whenever we play live, that big, fuck-off drum roll is going to be instantly recognizable as a bona fide Marvelous Beauhunk signature.

Who's the man?

Fucking right.

THE MBH TAKE THE FIFTH

October 1990

The Marvelous Beauhunks are now a five piece band.

Since our formation Steve's been shouldering most of the musical load. Not only has he been responsible for writing the music but he's rhythm and lead guitar player, back-up singer, and creator for Adam's minimal bass-lines. He's also limiting himself sound-wise, by playing a Rickenbacker, which isn't known for its ability to fill out the mid-range. Rickys are great for creating a fantastic jangly sound, but not so great for making a crunch. We want a fuller sound for playing live.

As we see it, our options are to have Glenn learn to play guitar as well as sing, replace Adam with a better bass player, or recruit a second guitarist from outside the band. The first two options don't sit well with me. Glenn's as much of a novice singer as Adam is bass player, so saddling him with something else to learn doesn't seem viable. Also Adam brings good chemistry to the group, so we can afford to give him more time to get control of his instrument. He's trying hard so that should count for something.

Auditioning new guitar players seems the most sensible route to go. Dan from M.I.U. is available and he was interested when I mentioned our recruitment plans. There's a style conflict with Dan's heavy metal background and our fascination with all things British and mod, so I was sure to be upfront with him as to the criteria we're after.

Looking the part's as important as making the right sounds, so he'd have to be willing to cut his hair and invest in the proper footwear.

Also, he'd have to get his hands on a guitar and amp better suited to our music than his current gear is.

Dan didn't think it would be a problem, so he checked us out at rehearsal, and decided to join up.

IN A WHITE ROOM

Saturday, November 17, 1990

Early Saturday morning, the newly revamped Marvelous Beauhunks load the gear into Adam's truck and make our way to White Room Studios in Whitby. We meet the engineer and owner of the studio, Scotty McClelland. Like an excited five-year-old, Glenn tells Scotty that he's been "waiting for this moment for 20 years."

Scotty nods patiently and says, "Great. Glad to hear it." He's seen all this before.

Scotty's older than us, about thirty-four. Steve's immediately put off by his "seventies classic rock" leanings. Steve figures there's no way this cat is going to pick up what the Marvelous Beauhunks are laying down. I'm just happy that we're finally in the studio so I'm not arsed one way or another.

The first order of business is to get the drums miked and the levels set. Scotty takes one look at my kit and asks me when I last changed the drum heads. Huh? I've never changed them. They look like they might be at least a decade old. He peeks inside my kick drum. Why is it lined with aluminium foil? I tell him I've read somewhere that John Bonham did the same thing to his drums to create a big bass sound.

Scotty shakes his head and mutters something under his breath. Three hours later, he declares the drums ready for recording although he won't be held responsible for them sounding like shite. "Next time, change the heads before recording," he says.

Next up is bass levels, and then getting the guitar amps ready. Glenn, sing into this mike . . .

La . . . la . . . . la . . . one-two, one-two . . . sibilance . . . bum-fun . . . one-two . . .

The clock's ticking so we work as quickly as possible recording the bed tracks to *TYNL* and *Dare to Dream*. Before long, my parts are done but not before I break the mike that's recording the snare drum, effectively blowing Scotty's profit margin for the weekend. The rest of the day is spent with guitar and bass overdubs, then lead and backing vocals. We've got a few tracks left over so I record some percussion for flavour.

Steve looks troubled. He pulls me aside. "Is that what we sound like? It doesn't sound much better than the four-tracking we did in the basement." I have to agree. Everything sounds flat and lifeless. All of a sudden, Scotty adds a gate to the snare drum and some reverb to the guitar. Everything pops out in Technicolor. Steve and I look at each other, amazed. Is that us?

Brilliant.

By the end of the first day, Scotty's had enough of us. Although we're excited beyond belief to be there, it's just another weekend job for him. Another set of broke, inexperienced kids, trying to cram all of their ideas into one session. I ask Scotty if he'd play back what we've recorded one last time before we wrap up. "I really don't want to . . ." is his response.

I'm sure as soon as we were out the door he was stuck into the pints. Afterwards, we spent a triumphant night at the Ozone while still making sure to stay energized for the morning. Sunday's going to be a big day spent mixing our songs.

WITH DARK CURTAINS

Sunday, November 18, 1990

Bright and early in the morning, we arrive at the studio holding takeout coffee, trying to keep our hands warm. It's a sunny, November Sunday and we're ready for business. Scotty opens the door looking bleary-eyed and grumpy. Yesterday must've done a bigger number on him than I originally thought.

We make our way to the control room and Scotty loads the reel-to-reel onto the tape machine. He starts with *Dare to Dream*. The kick drum is isolated and Scotty works the EQ's . . . thump, thump, thump, thump . . .

Eventually, we get bored and the chatter starts among us. Four of us are crammed onto the couch while Adam sits on the floor. Scotty's doing his best to work through the distraction until he's had enough and asks us to go watch TV in the other room so he can concentrate. When he's got enough of the mix completed, we'll be allowed to come back in to fine tune our ideas. Things like bringing up the guitars or making the backing vocals sound airier.

When we listen to the playback, I'm amazed at how good we sound. Dan has added some nice harmonies and some chicken-pickin' guitar that hadn't been there in rehearsal. Steve's parts are great and even Adam sounds good. The thing that really blows me away is the fact that Glenn can actually hold a tune.

We start the mixing process again with *TYNL*, but we run out of time to finish the job. Scotty marks down the fader moves onto the log sheet and we shelve it until the next session. The ride home is spent listening to *Dare to Dream* repeatedly on the car stereo, making sure that the mix translates well from the big studio monitors. Then several more plays on the stereo in Adam's room. It's very cool.

From that first weekend in the studio, I learned a lot about musical arrangements. I learned to stay quiet during the verses in order to create room for the singer and I learned how to play it straight when someone else was doing a solo. When the chorus came up, it was my turn to unload.

I thoroughly enjoyed being in the studio and despite what Scotty may think about us, I think he's a stand up guy.

I can't wait to go back.

Fantastic.

RETURN OF THE FABULOUS BOHUNKS

Saturday, December 22, 1990

"Thank you very much . . ."

Glenn wipes his brow on his sleeve and takes a pull on his Carlsberg. There are loud shouts of applause and encouragement. Steve casually tunes his guitar. Our singer is clearly in his element playing rock star, "This next one is called . . . *Blues From a Gun* . . . One, two, three, four . . ."

Tonight, we're playing a rocking return engagement at Pizza Pino's just in time for Christmas. With colleges and universities out for the term, the time is right for us to pack the room with family and friends. Cigarettes and drinks are consumed at a record pace and this time the poster correctly reads "the Marvelous Beauhunks." Playing on the bill with us is another Oshawa-based, psychedelic trio called the Mindset.

Whatever confidence we may have lost at Steve's wedding reception has been regained and we're performing our first headlining gig on solid footing. Somehow, we've managed to learn enough songs to play two full sets, which for us is a remarkable achievement.

Having Dan in the band has started to create some tension. He's been missing too many rehearsals. Adam in particular doesn't like having Dan around. Dan had played Adam's bass during practice when Adam was gone to Edmonton for two weeks. When Adam found out, he threw a fit like a pre-teen girl, while the rest of us laughed at him and took the piss. Steve started pouring it on how Dan was such a great bass player and how the band had never sounded better with Adam gone.

Unfortunately for Dan though, his lack of preparation is obvious during the show. He's falling behind and keeps looking over at Steve for the chord changes. Steve positions himself ever so slightly so that Dan only sees his back and not his guitar.

Despite all the accolades we received tonight, we're seething when the show ends. Dan made us look like cunts and almost ruined the gig. Adam seems almost a little too happy to be on the right side of the carnage for a change.

A friend of ours, self-styled hipster Derek Supryka, did the sound for us and has offered to manage the band. We don't think we really need a manager at this point but Derek's got a degree in music management from the Harris Institute and he can talk the talk. He says we're wasting our time with these small-potatoes gigs and he can get us some primo shows on Queen Street. Derek keeps talking about Brian Epstein and how we could be his Beatles, although I don't really see how that would work.

When we pack up to go home, and despite the blood in the water, we tell Dan "good show" and "see you at practice after Christmas." He has no idea that on this cold December night, in the parking lot of Pizza Pino's, that the chill running down his spine is the four of us conspiratorially treading over his musical grave.

Happy Holidays (from the most gutless band in the world).

SET LIST

Saturday, December 22, 1990

TYNL—Marvelous Beauhunks
Run Run Run—the Who
Kickin' Around—Marvelous Beauhunks
City Asleep—Marvelous Beauhunks
We Gotta Get Out of This Place—the Animals
Like Wow—Wipeout—Hoodoo Gurus
Happy Together—the Jam
Debbie Jones—Squire
My Mind Goes Round In Circles—Squire
Dare to Dream—Marvelous Beauhunks
Fantasy Merry-Go-Round—Marvelous Beauhunks
Heart Full of Soul—the Yardbirds
Pressure Drop—the Clash
Life From a Window—the Jam
What'd I Say?—Ray Charles
Money—the Beatles
Give Me More—Wonderstuff
Ready Steady Go—Generation X
Little Bitch—the Specials
Nice Legs (Shame About Her Face)—the Monks
What's All This Noise About Nothing?—Marvelous Beauhunks

THIS IS THE DAWNING OF A NEW ERA

January 1991

The sun shines and a new year beckons, offering promise and absolution. I could use a healthy dose of both.

In my family, the Christmas season is a lonely time. We sit around and stare, pretending we're normal and that we like each other. It's getting to be too much for me and I vow that one day soon I'll stop showing up. But this year I endured it.

Happily, a couple of weeks off seem to have done the Marvelous Beauhunks some good. We've regrouped fully engaged and brimming with enthusiasm. We've got plans to make and plans to execute (with "execute" being the operative word). Our first band meeting of the year is held upstairs at seven-eighty-two and, like the knights of Camelot, the four of us sit imperiously around the kitchen table.

Item one on the agenda—fire Dan. All in favour? Aye!

The ayes have it, motion carries.

Next up—who wants to do it?

Crickets chirping . . .

In an unheard of act of maturity, we decide that we're going do the right thing and have all four of us break the news to Dan . . . face-to-face. We bring him upstairs and tell him as nicely as we can that it isn't working out. It's not a personal thing. We like you and you're a good dude. We just realize that it's not feasible to take someone who's coming from an entirely different place musically, dress him up in a mod costume and expect that he's going to be into it as much as the rest of us.

Then we wait for Dan's reaction.

Dan surprises us. He's not that arsed about it. He's already decided to give us the boot, we just beat him to it. He thanks us for being up front and says that he's enjoyed playing with us. In fact, we've opened up a few more musical horizons for him. We shake hands and that's that.

Dan leaves and we're back to being a four-piece band.

We decide to stay that way.

MARVELOUS BEAUHUNKS PRESS-KIT

January 1991

The Marvelous Beauhunks, hailing from South Oshawa, started out together in February 1990. Steve Closs and Steve Wright got together to form the band, shortly thereafter recruiting bass player Adam Graham and lead singer Glenn Goodman.

Rather than classifying their sound in one particular category, the band prefers to let their audience decide for themselves. Although one can detect a distinct "British" flavour reminiscent of the '60s, in part due to their use of the vintage Rickenbacker guitar sound.

The Marvelous Beauhunks write their own material, influenced by such bands as the Yardbirds, the Clash, the Beatles, and the Jam. All members contribute to the creation of the band's musical direction and style.

Outside of music, the Marvelous Beauhunks pride themselves on being "the best-looking band in the world." Currently, the group are in the studio working on new material.

(Drawing—Stephen Wright)

RED DOG RAY

January 1991

"You get the door, ten percent of the bar and the Red Dog buffet. One portion of meat and all the potatoes you want."

Adam and I are in shock. Red Dog Ray beams magnanimously at us, his good deed for the day over with. Nudging me in the ribs, Adam takes me aside, "Do you realize that this means the more we drink, the more money we make?"

I nod in disbelief.

We're now booked for our fourth gig . . . Saturday, February 2, 1991 at the infamous Red Dog Tavern, located at Hunter Street West in Peterborough. Instead of the main stage upstairs, which is generally reserved for the more established acts, we're appearing downstairs in the Underdog where the alternative and college-rock groups play.

Late the previous night, Adam and I had agreed that, in the morning, we'd brave the blowing snow and leave seven-eighty-two, not to return home until we'd booked an out of town gig for the band.

Since Peterborough is Adam's old stomping ground from college, it seemed like the logical place to start. There's a high student population thanks to Trent University and Sir Sanford Fleming. If any town's going to be starved for hunky South Oshawa Brit-rock, then we bet that Peterborough's going to be the one. Adam said that the Red Dog Tavern's always been the best value for his money so he suggested we start there.

When we arrived at the Red Dog, we parked the truck and went in not knowing what to expect. This is Adam's turf, so he did the talking.

"Is Ray around?" he asked the first person that looked like they might have a clue.

Wait here.

Before long the man himself, Red Dog Ray McGregor, was standing before us, larger than life.

"What can I do for you boys?"

We gave Ray our pitch and tried to look confident. All the while, we silently prayed that Ray wouldn't ask us how many times we've played or how big our fan-base is.

"So how many times have you fellows played?" Ray asked thumbing through our scant press kit.

"Got a big following have you?"

Shit.

We tried to fumble our way around the facts while still maintaining some element of truth. Ray sized us up and cut through the crap. Getting out his calendar he said, "Tell you boys what. I'm gonna put you in on the Second of February . . . It's a Saturday. If you do a good job, we'll have you back. If you don't . . ." he shrugged and trailed off ominously.

Adam and I assured Ray that we'll pull in the numbers and that he won't regret it. Relax Ray, we're the Marvelous Beauhunks. Ray gave us a tour of the Underdog and showed us the two band rooms where we can sleep it off after the show.

We shake hands and thank Red Dog Ray for the gig. We try to appear nonchalant but all the while our minds are bubbling over.

To seal the deal, Ray offers us a trip up to the Red Dog buffet, on him. "One portion of meat and all the potatoes you want."

And now that our bellies are full and our mission's been accomplished, Adam and I leave the Red Dog behind and make our way along the slushy Hunter Street sidewalks, back to the truck.

We're on a roll. So what to do next?

Adam suggests that we make our way over to the Wire, a music and entertainment weekly, similar to Toronto's NOW Magazine or EYE Weekly. We can drop off our press kit and start plugging the show.

The good thing about small towns like Peterborough is that nobody seems to mind being dropped in on. I guess it helps to break up the daily routine. So when Adam and I appear unannounced in the second floor offices of the Wire, owner/publisher Michael Bell acts as though he's been expecting us.

A quick chat explaining our purpose elicits a promise of coverage from Michael, to appear the week before the show. He asks us some questions about the band's origins and listens to our demo of *Dare to Dream*. We spend some time learning about his musical past, especially his time as the singer for the '80s band, Eye Eye. Like we did with Ray, Adam and I shake hands with Michael and thank him for his time and support.

As we trudge down the stairs and back out onto the streets we're mystified. We don't know anyone who's both a working musician and a successful businessman. As far as we're concerned the two are mutually exclusive entities, diametrically opposed.

"What do you make of that?" I ask Adam.

"Corporate longhair," Adam replies dismissively.

"Yeah . . ." That makes sense.

We get back in the truck, satisfied with the days results, and head south on a snowy Highway 115 toward home.

Fucking boneheads.

ENTERTAINMENT SECTION

Peterborough Examiner—Wednesday, January 30, 1991

The Marvelous Beauhunks from Oshawa visit the Underdog Saturday.

The band—Steve Closs, Steve Wright, Adam Graham, and Glenn Goodman—formed about a year ago and perform all original material influenced by the likes of the Yardbirds, the Clash, the Beatles, and the Jam. There's a distinctive '60s flavour to their music, partly due to the band's vintage Rickenbacker guitar sound.

The Beauhunks pride themselves on being "the best-looking band in the world." Be your own judge.

GROUNDHOG DAY (LOADING OUT)

Saturday, February 2, 1991

"Jesus Christ Steve, you're white as a fucking ghost!"

I arrive home with a skip in my step from what seemed like a never-ending Saturday spent washing vegetables, and I'm looking forward to finally loading the truck and hitting the open road. It's Groundhog Day 1991. More importantly it's Underdog Day. The Four Horsemen of Rock Apocalypse are clamouring for their sacrifice and they will not be denied.

It's time to pay the rent . . .

Beauhunk style . . . .

Whatever that means.

Steve lays on the couch all pasty and pale, huddled beneath some heavy blankets. Between shivers he weakly assures me "I'm okay, man . . . just let me get my guitars . . ."

Oh fuck. This doesn't look good at all. At practice on Tuesday, Steve had shown up with a small sniffle. By Thursday's rehearsal, the sniffle had brought company; a hacking cough and a sore throat. Today, Steve can barely lift his head off the pillow.

Reacting to my look of panic, Steve croaks out, "Don't worry, I can still play the show . . ."

I nod sympathetically, hoping that my face doesn't betray the sinking feeling down in the pit of my stomach. Leaving Steve to recuperate, Adam and I bounce down the stairs to the basement and begin tearing down the PA. Mixing board—check. Mikes—check. Microphone stands, cables . . . check, check. We take my drum kit apart, pack the hardware into an old army duffle, and slide the cymbals into their specially padded bag. My snare has its own case. The rest of the drums are on their own and will have to weather the elements. Saved toward the end, we lift Adam's bass rig into the truck. We leave Steve's Fender Twin until very last. That amp, while not particularly intimidating in size, is incredibly heavy beyond belief. More than once, I've suspected that Steve might be hiding a small jar of Mercury in its base as ballast.

Surveying the practice space to ensure that nothing important gets left behind, I find that the room looks strange without its normal clutter. Imprints of amplifiers and mike stands crease the low-pile greenish-coloured carpet. In the back corner where I spend my time hunched over my drums, lays several broken drum sticks and the floor's littered with wood shavings. As happy as I am to be out gigging, I can't help but feel a hint of melancholy at leaving the room to sit quiet and empty. It's as if, by removing our equipment, we've stripped our big red house of its energy and spirit.

Out in the driveway, Adam and I finish with the last of the heavy lifting. Glenn and Cathy pull up, with Derek strapped into the backseat of Glenn's car. He's working as soundman for the show tonight. We take the piss out of Glenn and call him a calculating bastard for not showing up in time to help out with the load. After one final check we're ready to roll. Adam and I follow Glenn onto the eastbound ramp of the 401 and eventually we point our caravan northward on the 115, toward Peterborough. Adam and I drive the gear in the truck, while the prostrate Steve and his precious Rickenbackers ride with Damyana.

This is our first band-on-the-road experience, and even though Steve's under the weather and two band wives are in tow, it's one of those magical moments that come along once in a young musician's life.

Eric Burdon and the Animals are providing a comforting, soulful, distraction, as Adam and I smoke cigarettes and pass the drive with nervous chatter about set lists, sound checks, and groupies. Especially groupies.

I think I'm going to like this rock 'n' roll business . . .

GROUNDHOG DAY (THE OPENING BAND)

Saturday, February 2, 1991

"THAT's the Marvelous Beauhunks . . . ?!? Let's get out of here . . ."

Adam and I watch in dismay as the two cute co-eds enter and then immediately exit the Underdog. They're shaking their heads instead of their asses. We try to tell them that it's the Mindset onstage not the Marvelous Beauhunks, but we're not fast enough.

Fuck.

Things aren't going well for the Mindset. Since they're the only band we know, we've asked them to play support for us again. At the top of their set, the singer made some disparaging remarks about playing in the sticks and may have implied something about the dangers of inbreeding. We saw first hand just how easily a crowd can turn on you, and when they do there's no getting them back.

That was strike one.

For some reason, they've ignored the earlier warning of the Red Dog's manager. During sound check, she told them to turn down the amps. Now, they're playing at a thoroughly obnoxious volume even by punk standards. Beneath the din of guitar and bass, the drums, which are usually the loudest instrument, can barely be heard.

That's strike two.

Now the manager's back and yelling at us to get them to "turn it down or turn it off." The Mindset's overpowering the band on the main stage, local Peterborough boys "Bandanna with Dennis O'Toole." The punters upstairs like their country music and they won't put up with any bullshit from some short-haired hippies from the city. If they don't turn down the racket, the plug will be pulled and we'll be blacklisted.

That's strike three.

I'm pissed. No way is some other band going to blow this gig for us. As soon as they finish their song, Derek cuts power to the PA. Steve and Adam invade the stage to adjust the amps. Steve, sick as he is, is spoiling for action. It's his Fender Twin that the guitar player's been pushing to the point of nuclear meltdown.

Discretion, rather than tangling with a sweaty, infectious, guitar-player, turns out to be the better part of valour and the Mindset finish their lower-volume set without further incident. When it's over, they down tools and drift off into the background. Adam slips a tape of Booker T and the MG's into the sound system and the mood in the room lightens considerably.

Fucking musicians.

GROUNDHOG DAY (MARVELOUS BEAUHUNKS)

Saturday, February 2, 1991

"Thanks for coming out tonight. For those of you who don't know us, we're the Marvelous Beauhunks from South Oshawa . . . . hit it . . ."

Weak-kneed but bravely on his feet, Everton football scarf protecting his swollen glands, Steve plunges into his chugging guitar riff with its stuttering, start-stop pattern as we kick off our set with that barn-burning, lyrical embarrassment, *TYNL*.

I feel tight but calm and hit my cue with an energetic crack. I crash and splash away to my heart's content. Taking in the Underdog from my drummer's vantage point I revel in the curious mixture of faux-wood paneling, Z-BRICK and graffiti. I notice that Toronto cowpunks, the Absolute Whores, have played here recently. They've seen fit to proudly spray-paint their name on the wall to my left, directly over my monitor wedge. Yee-Haw.

A steady stream of punters are moving and mingling while we play. Some of them we know from Oshawa, friends that made the trip up the 115 with us. Other friends are students at the university and they've talked their friends into coming to the show. There are even a few geezers who've appeared based on the posters we've hung around town—cartoon effigies of the band advertising "'60s style rock 'n' roll played by the Best-Looking Band in the World! for $2 at the door."

If I ever doubted that we're in the midst of cottage country, trespassers in the land of Kim Mitchell, where nobody hurts and nobody dies, that feeling disappears as I examine the lighting rig surrounding the stage area. Situated over Glenn's head and bathing him in a pastel glow is nothing more than a string of coloured patio lanterns hanging low from the ceiling. Adam and I make eye contact and exchange a moment of hysterical laughter at the absurdity of the situation.

But we've made good on our word to Red Dog Ray and have drawn a respectable crowd. The business back at the bar is moving at a brisk pace. As Adam predicted, our ten percent of the liquor proceeds should prove to be lucrative. After we pay off the Mindset, I look forward to a having a few extra dollars in my trousers thanks to tonight. I might be able to afford food as well as cigarettes next week. It seems too good to be true.

I allow myself a moment of pride. We've worked hard to fill the room tonight by strong-arming promises of attendance from anyone and everyone we could think of. Hundreds of flyers have been stapled and pasted to lamp-posts and doorways, despite the brutal Kawartha winter. Visits to local newspapers like the Trent Arthur and the Peterborough Examiner, pushing for coverage were handled by Adam and me. It was hard work and we've pulled it off. The punters are having a blast and the band is playing full-on, especially Steve, who's drawing energy from some untapped reservoir within himself. Glenn, of course is charming. Even Adam is wiggling his bum a bit.

We eventually burn through every song we know plus a few that we still aren't sure about. Twenty-two songs in total including *Like Wow—Wipe Out* by the Hoodoo Gurus, a ska version of *Nice Legs (Shame About Her Face)* by the Monks, as well as *Happy Together* by the Jam. We cram in our own marvelous originals wherever they fit. After four encores we had to give up, only because we've resorted to a twenty minute version of *Gloria* by Them and you can only tread on that one for so long.

E-E-D-A . . . E-E-D-A . . . Glo-ria . . . . G-L-O-R-I-A . . . Glo-ria . . .

When the crowd dissipates, Derek, Steve, Glenn, Adam, and I pose for some post-gig photos looking sweaty, giddy, drunk, and exhausted.

The rent is paid in full.

The Four Horsemen agree. They're well pleased.

GROUNDHOG DAY
(THE MORNING AFTER)

Sunday, February 3, 1991

"Here, Sticks," says Steve handing me three bills. "Your cut from last night . . ."

Sixty dollars.

In my booze-addled cranium, I calculate a quick mental inventory.

Let's see . . . I played my drums well and was heroically lionized for it. Many trips to the bar and spartan lodgings were provided to the band, free of charge. Company for the evening had been easy to find.

According to my calculations, the only freight I'm paying for this introduction to rock and roll hedonism is a headache brought on by dehydration, and a tongue that feels too big for my mouth. By my way of thinking, it's a very fair trade.

Behind the Underdog, in the cold, painful light of morning stands Red Dog Ray, smiling and solicitous. We're loading our gear into the truck. He's satisfied with the bar receipts from last night, courtesy of the best-looking band in the world. Ray hands Steve a small bundle of bills, which Steve thumbs through efficiently. He pulls three twenties for each of us.

Sixty dollars? Fuck off. I know I'd have paid Red Dog Ray $60 just for the night out. And I'd call that a bargain. The best I ever had.

Blinking hard and unable to produce anything other than syrupy Black Label tears, I fight the urge to weep uncontrollably. You big, beautiful, bald-headed, red-dog-mountain-man. The world can be a kind and wonderful place after all.

Unfortunately, I don't have the opportunity to dwell on such deep musings. I need to get home and go to sleep before I throw up in Adam's truck.

Beauhunk-style . . .

PICTURES AND TEARS

February 1991

"I wrote a new song. It's called *Pictures and Tears*. It's about my granny."

Is he winding us up? Glenn's usually so laid-back that it's not always clear when he's taking the piss.

"C'mon Glenn, are you taking the fucking piss?"

"No man, my gran just died and I'm pretty bummed out about it . . . . Seriously."

Standing behind the mike, stylishly turned out in tan desert boots, immaculate quiff, and a black t-shirt sporting the Sun Records logo, Glenn gently pulls a sheet of folded note paper from the front pocket of his Levis. Scribed in his meticulous block printing are the words to the sixth song in the tome of Marvelous Beauhunk originals. I take a look at his lyrics. Not bad Glenn. Not bad at all.

But your grandmother? That's just too fucking weird. No one besides Glenn would write a fucking pop song about their Nan. Well, Elvis Costello did it. But I mean, apart from him, who does this?

. . . *And her name was Veronica* . . .

As Glenn explains it, he's always been close to his granny back in England and over the past while she's had a slow, downward turn in her health which culminated in a state of dementia. She hadn't recognized her family near the end and this is weighing heavily on him.

This is the moment that Glenn becomes a fully three-dimensional human being to me. Up until then, I've had him summed up as nothing more than a fun-loving, good-looking git who had the world by the ass and, unlike me, was impervious to life's sucker-punches and cheap kidney shots.

Alright mate, if you want to sing about your Nan, then I'm cool with it. Deal me in.

Adam, in his combination of dry, acerbic wit and social ineptitude, quips "Hey Glenn, instead of *Pictures and Tears*, why don't you call it *Nana's Gone Bananas . . . ?*"

Glenn doesn't crack so much as a smile. I, on the other hand, nearly wet my trousers and join Adam, who's doubled over with laughter.

I know it's wrong and insensitive of us to make fun of Glenn's song about his grandma.

But you've gotta admit . . . Adam's joke is at least a *little bit* funny.

FANTASY MERRY-GO-ROUND (DAY 1)

Saturday, February 23, 1991

Strapped into clunky headphones and Paul Weller rock-star shades, Steve's head bops up and down in time with the Madchester beat of *Fantasy Merry-Go-Round*. Condenser mikes peak as they struggle to keep up with his strumming. From behind the mixing desk, Scotty and I watch Steve through the glass. We glance at each other and nod. Pressing down the talk-back button, Scotty shouts, "That's a take! C'mon back in and have a listen."

With Steve's overdubs complete, the recording of *Fantasy Merry-Go-Round* grinds to a halt on Saturday night, February 23, 1991. It's too late for us to make last call at the Ozone. Of the 16 tracks we've got to work with, Steve's used six of them for guitar. When he originally tried to explain to Scotty why he needed six guitar tracks, Scotty got that "Here we go again" look on his face. But as the song began to take shape, Scotty was surprised to find us better prepared and more musically sophisticated than we'd been four months ago.

Although we still don't know how to articulate what we're trying for, our mod-punk-ska roots are beginning to show themselves in our approach to recording. All we've got are our instincts and we're relying on Scotty to provide the rudder. Steve's begun to forgive Scotty his advanced age and penchant for musician's music and we're beginning to collaborate. Good things are happening.

While Glenn and Adam are amusing themselves with reruns of the Simpsons in the other room, the three of us map out the game-plan for the rest of the weekend. Our goal is to push hard to complete an entry for CFNY's Modern Music Search. Recently, we've brought

Derek on board as our manager and his first order of business is for us to finish something in time for the contest deadline on March 8th.

Derek's strategy is a good one. CFNY's been championing a band called the Barenaked Ladies, who are managed by an associate of Derek's. As a result of being on last year's CFNY Modern Music disc, they're selling out the best clubs in Toronto. Rumour has it that the record companies are circling like sharks, ready to snap them up. All this for what's basically a novelty act.

Wait until they see what's emerging 58 kilometres to the east.

It's time for a revolution.

FANTASY MERRY-GO-ROUND (DAY 2)

Sunday, March 3, 1991

The mix for *Fantasy Merry-Go-Round* turned out well. It's got a great energy and vibe to it. All we need to do now is get Adam to redo his bonking bass-line for *TYNL* and we'll be able to remix it too.

Three hours later . . .

All Adam has to show for his efforts are sore fingers, a bruised ego, and an ultimatum. Get bass lessons or you're out.

We mix what we can salvage, but we haven't seen the last of *TYNL* in the studio.

DARE TO DREAM (RE-MIX)

Monday, March 4, 1991

We've decided to upgrade the mix of *Dare to Dream* from the quarter-inch analogue version that we did in November. This means doing another mix onto the studio's new DAT machine.

The results are good and *Dare to Dream's* become a contender for our entry into the Modern Music Search contest.

WAITING FOR THE MAN(AGER)

Tuesday, March 5, 1991

Since early February, Derek's been working hard to book us into the downtown Toronto market. His toolbox consists of nothing more than our three song demo, a few black and white stills, and our history of three performances, not counting Steve's wedding. Still he manages to spin us as the second coming of Christ.

As our manager, Derek occasionally comes to rehearsals. He likes to check out the music and hang out. Tonight, he seems preoccupied like there's something troubling him. He rummages through his Filofax and poses a rhetorical question.

"What band is playing at Stratengers on Sunday, April 7th?"

All of a sudden the room is quiet except for the buzzing of the PA.

"That's great fucking news . . . way to go man!"

Before the high-fiving and back-slapping starts, Derek continues to thumb his Filofax. He pauses and poses another rhetorical question.

"What band is playing the legendary El Mocambo on Tuesday, April 9th as part of an independent showcase?"

Our jaws drop. Glenn drools. The high-fiving and back-slapping take place in earnest. The El Mocambo. We can't believe it.

One last rhetorical question is put forward by our more-valuable-by-the-minute manager.

"Now, which band is auditioning on Sunday, March 10th to open for the Byrds at the Purple Onion?"

"That's right, you guys are . . ."

Derek Supryka with Ray Davies from the Kinks
(Photo—Derek Supryka Collection)

TIME HAS COME TODAY

Wednesday, March 6, 1991

The clock finally runs out and thumbs its nose. There's two days left to submit our entry to CFNY. We pace the White Room with wooden ears and listen to our newly-minted songs. We have one shot at this—we've got to make it count.

"I dunno. What d'you think Steve?" I ask.

"I dunno. What d'you think Glenn?" Steve replies.

"I dunno. What d'you think Steve?" Glenn asks me.

"I dunno. What d'you think Adam?" I ponder.

"Who cares what Adam thinks," interjects Steve.

In the time-honoured spirit of band democracy, we can't decide on anything.

Typical.

Fucking.

Idiot.

Musicians.

THIS CHARMING MAN

Friday, March 8, 1991

We're in a ground floor cafeteria, nestled between the Gardiner Expressway and Queen's Quay. Hunched around a small table, Glenn, Derek and I are filling out a bundle of forms. It's the last day that CFNY will accept submissions and we're cutting it close.

Ten minutes ago we were on the 25th floor of the Toronto Star Building in the wood-panelled corporate sales offices of CFNY, 102.1 FM. The cute receptionist gave us a copy of the contest rules and told us to take them down to the coffee-shop. Glenn smiled at her. She smiled at him. I hated and admired Glenn all at the same time.

Derek reads out the particulars of the blue-coloured papers in front of us, while I fill in the blanks. The rules are straightforward. Are we an unsigned band? Yes. Is our song under five minutes in length? Yes. It's three-minutes and twenty-seven seconds long. Do we have an eight-by-ten photo of the band with bio? Yes. Glenn looks particularly handsome in this shot.

With a spot on the disc will come exposure and airplay. Winners will perform at a CFNY sponsored showcase at the Copa and one band will be chosen to play at Molson Park on Canada Day. CFNY will send copies of the disc to campus radio stations all over North America.

As of 5 p.m. today, all submissions will be in the hands of a CFNY panel and the top 10 songs will be picked based on creativity, performance, marketability, and production quality. It's anticipated that between 300-400 applicants will be submitting songs this year.

We're feeling confident. On our way down to CFNY, we stopped at a studio belonging to some of Derek's friends. The Daddys of Eden were the number three spot on last year's disc with the song *Junk for Jesus*. They figure we have a legitimate shot.

The paperwork's done.

It's time to pay the rent.

We hold our breath as the elevator takes us up twenty-five stories. No matter what happens, it's a calculated risk. All our deliberating in the studio yielded no last minute epiphanies. Before we left for Toronto, Steve called me from work and mumbled *Fantasy-Merry-Go-Round* into the phone, so that's the song we're submitting.

I hand over the completed forms, our photo, and the tape to the cute receptionist. I cross my fingers.

"Good luck you guys," she says, looking only at Glenn.

"Thanks," says Glenn, he of the charming smile.

"What the fuck is it with you?" I ask him once we're on the elevator.

We drive back to Oshawa, away from the setting sun. The CN Tower is silhouetted on the horizon as we travel through the Toronto traffic. As we clear the junction where Eastern Avenue meets Kingston Road, the Daddys of Eden come on the radio.

We all agree that it's a good omen.

EIGHT MILES HIGH

Saturday, March 9, 1991

It's Saturday morning at the supermarket and I'm shaking away the cobwebs. It's my job to stack the front display with ripe yellow bananas. I'm tired, cranky and fearful of banana spiders. The only way for me to get through today's tedium is to put yesterday out of my mind. No more rock-star dreams. It's time to pay the rent for real.

Besides, Sunday's another big day.

We're auditioning to open for the Byrds.

EIGHT MILES LOW

Sunday, March 10, 1991

"Alright, now play a ballad . . ."

Huh . . . ?!

I look at Adam and Adam looks at me. We look at each other and then we look at Steve.

What the fuck is he doing?

Duh, duh, duh, duh . . . duh, duh, duh, duh . . .

Tell me he's not playing the Jam's classic *Life From a Window* at half speed?

Steve looks over at me, nodding for me to join in.

Fuck me, he is.

Steve hovers on his G chord, playing down-strokes, waiting for me to mirror his eighth-notes on my snare and hi-hats.

Duh, duh, duh, duh . . . duh, duh, duh, duh . . .

I join in. Then Adam. I fucking hope Steve knows what he's doing.

Glenn starts to sing, sounding like a record set to the wrong speed . . .

I've got a bad feeling about this.

We've never played a fucking ballad before in our lives and it's certainly never been placed on the agenda for any of our weekly band meetings. Did I miss a memo? Adam looks at me like he might've missed the memo too. Still, I've to give Steve credit for pulling this one out of his arse though. We want this show very, very badly.

Before we finish the song, the tempo's almost back to full speed and the jig is up. The Purple Onion manager waves us off the stage.

"Ok guys, good job . . . that's enough . . ."

Derek asks him, "What do you think? Great huh? I guess that means we've got the gig . . ."

In Derek's mind, aside from the pseudo-ballad, we've nailed the audition. He's never heard us play better. The gig is ours.

"Yeah, that really wasn't a ballad . . . but the other songs you guys played were good. You've got some nice background vocals happening and some good energy . . . but you really shouldn't be playing a Rickenbacker . . . you need to play a Gibson SG . . . that'd really make your guitar solos stand out. Yeah. The crowd for the Byrds is going to be a bit older and they're going to want to dance to some slow songs. Yeah. I don't think you guys are quite ready yet . . . why don't you come back in six months after you've done some more gigs and give it another try."

Fuck, fuck, fuck, fuck, fuck . . . .

Derek tells the Purple Onion manager that he's wrong and that the band is up to the task. I'm impressed by how calm and professional Derek comes across. The rest of us stand there and keep it buttoned. I'm surprised that Steve doesn't pop off. The Gibson SG comment is something he's liable to take personally. We pack our gear and make tracks.

Screw you man.

Back at seven-eighty-two, we mope around the basement, fronting and talking tough. It's not even the original Byrds for-fuck-sake. There's no David Crosby or Roger McGuinn. Who needs to play some poxy gig in Oshawa anyway? We're playing the fucking El Mocambo. We're the Marvelous Beauhunks and we don't fucking care.

But we do care. This little set-back cuts into the band's collective body armour way more than any of us lets on.

Fuck.

HERE COMES RICHARD

Sunday, March 31, 1991

Steve and Damyana have moved out of seven-eighty-two and into their own house.

At first, we were concerned. A new tenant on the main floor of seven-eighty-two means that we lose access to the basement and, subsequently, our rehearsal space.

Somehow Steve's managed to convince his co-worker, Richard, that he'll "let" him take over the flat. The condition is that Richard will continue to allow us to rehearse on Tuesdays and Thursdays, and any other days we deem "necessary."

Miraculously, Richard has been agreeable to these conditions and he dutifully vacates his new home from 7 to 9 p.m. twice a week. He's never complained about his increased electricity bill from our gear and we've neglected to offer Richard any compensation.

As an added bonus, Damyana's no longer around to complain about the noise.

KILL WHITEY

Sunday, April 7, 1991

I lug my kick drum through the side door and hump it up to the stage. Something's making Adam clutch his sides and howl with laughter. I squint to see what's so funny.

In contrast to the bright sunlight that's making Toronto so unseasonably warm for so early in April, the atmosphere inside Stratengers is comparatively muted and dark. It takes my eyes a few seconds to adjust. By now, Adam is nearing hysterics, pointing toward something on the wall. His torso is heaving.

I look upward, forcing my eyes into focus, desperate to get in on the joke. Blurriness gives way to lucidity and I stand there, waiting to be swept away with laughter.

All I can see is a dirty, beige, album cover hanging on the wall, showing a Native American wearing a feathered headpiece. He's on a horse and brandishing a spear. Fuck, Adam. That's not funny—that's just racist.

I take a closer look. Oh, my.

In blue, ball-point pen, some thoughtful patron has seen fit to draw a cartoon-like, word-bubble shouting out from the majestic Native American's mouth.

"Kill Whitey!"

"Jesus Christ," I think, and I'm stunned into a ponderous silence.

Tear are streaming from his eyes as Adam lights a cigarette and walks away. He's shaking his head and muttering to himself, "Kill Whitey . . . ahahaaahahaaa . . ."

Record covers notwithstanding, our big night at Stratengers is a low-key affair. We're playing to a near-empty room, so we use the opportunity to build some confidence and stretch out on a bigger stage. It's a good chance for us to get used to a professional sound system.

Sharing the bill with us are some of Derek's friends, a funk-rock band called the Life. They're more experienced than we are and come across as more polished. I begin to think that we could be in trouble until their guitar player spins around and does the splits. That makes me feel better.

The Stratengers show isn't a life changing event, but it's earned us our first badge of credibility in establishing ourselves as a Queen Street band. It might be the wrong end of Queen Street but at least now we've occupied the same real estate as the Waltons, and the Saddle Tramps.

With the El Mocambo coming up in two days, we won't be in Sunday night purgatory for long.

Glenn Goodman, Adam Graham at Stratengers
(Photo—Adam Graham Collection)

YOU MAY ASK YOURSELF

Tuesday, April 9, 1991

How did I get here?

"Alright . . . welcome to the El Mocambo . . . we are the Marvelous Beauhunks from Oshawa, the city that Moto-vates Canada. Do you feel mo-to-vated?"

A drunken shout signals the affirmative. We're backlit in multicolour on the stage and we're ready to attack. Taking up the wall behind us is a large, blue-skied, palm-treed "El Mocambo" mural.

I count us in, stomp my kick pedal and assault my snare with both sticks. Steve responds with his jangly guitar intro . . .

Here in the darkness, it's three-forty-five now . . .
In my city asleep . . .
Here in my city asleep . . .

"Unbelievable." I muse.

It's only our fifth gig and we're playing on the same stage that Elvis Costello and the Attractions did back in March 1978. Sure the Rolling Stones recorded *Love You Live* here in 1977, but to me Elvis is the money-shot. As of right now, there's nothing else in the world that I need to accomplish.

After *City Asleep* comes *My Mind Goes Round in Circles.* We follow it with a punked-up *Heart Full of Soul.* Adam is in a near-catatonic state of Stones-worship and he channels his best Keef Richards. He's misplaced his musical limitations tonight and he's locked in tight with my drums.

Not even our billing as the "Marvelous Bohunks" can dampen our spirits. We're too overcome with the idea that we're walking the same stage that the Ramones, Johnny Thunders, and Black Flag have done before us. We know the stories of cross-country tours in the backs of vans, non-existent per diems, and the steady diet of stale beer and cigarettes. All done for the glory of appearing on your own album cover. This is what we want too.

By the time we perform our obligatory thrashing of *Fantasy Merry-Go-Round,* our thirteen-song-set is nearly finished. With the last notes of *Little Bitch*, we reluctantly give over the stage to the headlining band, a likeable but style-challenged, trio called the Fact.

As we clear the backline, Derek congratulates us on a job well done.

"The promoter really likes us. He thinks we'll be a good act to play support for Havana 3AM at the Spectrum next month," enthuses Derek using the affectation "we" when referring to the band, causing Steve's eyebrow to raise.

Havana 3AM is the Latino-rockabilly group formed by the coolest man to strap on a bass, ex-Clash member Paul Simonon. They're doing a club tour of North America on the back of their new single *Reach the Rock*. We can't believe our good luck.

The five of us grab some beer from the bar and smugly settle in to see what the Fact have in store for us. The gods of rock may be working our corner tonight, but it soon becomes apparent that they've forsaken the Fact. Aside from us and some staff from the supermarket where Derek and I work, the club is now a ghost-town. As soon as we finished our set, people started leaving and now tumbleweeds are rolling through the El Mocambo.

Suddenly we're magnanimous and we decide to give the Fact our complete attention. Between songs we're overly-generous with our applause. I find it especially easy to be noble when I'm feeling self-satisfied. Now would be a good time to ask me to sponsor a third-world child.

Eventually, we all end up on the dance floor as the Fact grind through covers of the Cult and Steppenwolf. The assistant manager of the supermarket falls on his ass without spilling a drop of his beer. He springs back up and keeps dancing like it never happened.

Before the Fact's set is over, Glenn manages to land himself a job at the supermarket too.

Upon returning to seven-eighty-two, Adam and I are stuck with the load-in. "It must be a rhythm-section thing, to get fucked over when there's heavy lifting," I lament to Adam.

We trudge upstairs and make our way to our respective bedrooms. The answering-machine blinks on the desk outside my door. I press the button and listen to the message that comes out of the tinny, single-mono, speaker.

"Adam, get out here," I shout frantically. I hit another button and the tape squelches, rewinding itself.

Adam, concerned that there's something wrong, skids down the hall.

I hit the "play" button again and this is what we hear.

"Hey guys, this is Hal Harbour, Director of Canadian Music Development at CFNY. I've got your tape of Fantasy-Merry-Go-Round and I'd like to get the band in the studio for an interview as soon as possible. Call me back."

Life as we know it is about to change.

Stephen Closs at the El Mocambo
(Photo—Adam Graham Collection)

Stephen Closs, Glenn Goodman at the El Mocambo
(Photo—Adam Graham Collection)

PART 2
CFNY

Wednesday, April 10, 1991

Derek called for the second time this morning. We're all excited about last night's message. It's like being "discovered" in a Hollywood drugstore in the fifties.

"We're booked for tomorrow afternoon at 2," he says.

Hal Harbour's assistant, Joanne Faloona, has arranged for us to be interviewed at CFNY's Kennedy Road studios in Brampton.

"But I have to work tomorrow," I say, crestfallen. "Can't we do it another day?"

"Sorry, Wrighty," Derek replies. "She says it's got to be tomorrow."

Somehow, I've become "Wrighty" when it comes to band matters.

This is a drag. Steve won't be able to go either. He's not going to be happy when he finds out that Adam will be going and he won't be. I try not to be too disappointed. I have to admit that I'm a little concerned that Glenn will be left unchecked.

Later when I leave home to go out, my car won't start. It's either the battery or the alternator, or both. It's a bad time for a car repair. My sister's getting married on Friday and I'm already out of pocket for a tuxedo rental.

Glenn shows up out of the blue and helps me push my car to the garage at the corner of Simcoe and Wentworth. He hasn't been employed since the half day he spent as a lawn-sprayer. He says he was sacked for backing the truck into a tree.

As we hump my car down the street, we talk about tomorrow's interview.

Who knew that becoming rock stars was going to be this easy?

Thursday, April 11, 1991

Derek says the interview went well and that Glenn did a good job. Adam was given some questions too, but he flubbed them. Hal asked him who his bass influences were, so Adam told him "Jaco Pastorius".

Jaco Pastorius!

Adam also tried saying Paul Simonon from the Clash, but he couldn't pronounce his name.

Hahahahaha . . . .

Friday, April 12, 1991

My sister married "Gorilla" Phil today.

I'm persona non-grata at St. Mary's Catholic church. Just because I asked the priest, "Why is there water in the ashtrays?"

Jesus Christ—get a sense of humour.

CFNY SPOTLIGHT—THE STREETS OF ONTARIO

Sunday, April 14, 1991

Hal Harbour:

"That's the Marvelous Beauhunks from CFNY 102.1, Fantasy Merry-Go-Round.

I had a chance to chat with lead vocalist, Glenn Goodman, from the Marvelous Beauhunks, and like I always do, I kind of wondered about the band name."

Glenn Goodman:

"Well actually it's kind of funny because when we first got the band going we were in the Tartan.

That's a pub in Oshawa.

It was St. Patrick's Day last year, and we were kind of boozing it up and we were just throwing around names.

We were called the 782'ers at first because that's the address where they lived, right, and we didn't like that so we were just throwing around names and then someone, I don't even remember who it was, just said, 'What about the Beauhunks?'

And somebody said, 'How about the MARVELOUS Beauhunks?' And we all went 'Yeah! That's the one!' So there's not really any sort of meaning behind it.

That's just the way it is."

WE'RE NUMBER TWO

Monday, April 15, 1991

"Steve Wright—Phone call on line one. Steve Wright line one."

It's never a good sign to get a phone call at work.

I use the phone in the back of the seafood department. It smells like detergent, ammonia and the ocean. Half-dead lobsters are staring back at me.

"Hello?" I ask tentatively.

"Hi, Stephen. It's Joanne Faloona from CFNY," says the chirpy girl on the phone.

"Congratulations! You guys have been chosen to be on this year's CFNY Modern Music disc. You didn't make the top 10, but we want to put you guys on as a bonus track. You're going to be the second song on the disc."

Silence.

"So are you excited?" asks Joanne.

"Can you call Derek?" I respond. "He's our manager."

I sound like a dick.

When I go back to the produce department, I'm in a daze. I explain to my coworkers that my band has just been given a once-in-a-lifetime opportunity.

"That's great Steve-o, I'm really happy for you," says my boss Verne. "I really am."

"But right now we've got potatoes to stack."

THE MARQUEE, TORONTO—w/ Mindset, Heebee Gee

Tuesday, April 16, 1991

The Mindset owe us a couple of shows, so they've invited us to play the Marquee at the corner of Coxwell and Gerrard. Derek's relayed this info to Hal's assistant, Joanne, and they're coming to check us out live.

Since Steve still gets anxious before shows, the rest of us have decided not to tell him that we're being critiqued by CFNY's hitmakers.

At the last minute, the Mindset call and tell us not to come. Before any *Beauhunk-style* revenge can be planned, we decide to show up ready to play anyway. There's too much at stake.

The Mindset are surprised to see us arrive. Derek corrals the club manager, a biker by the name of "Ratch", and he pleads our case.

"We were invited to play and then uninvited at the last minute. We don't think that's fair."

Ratch looks like he could care less if we live or die, let alone play the gig. He prints up some tickets for us and we're the "MARV SLOUS BEAUHUNKS" for the night.

The Marquee's empty save for the bands, Derek, and our friends Sheila and Jenn. When Hal and Joanne show up, they're with Massimo, who was part of the selection process for the disc. Derek plays host while we're on stage. Hal tells Jenn that we've got a lot of potential.

Between songs, Glenn says into the microphone, “I’d like to thank our friends from CFNY for coming out to see us tonight.”

Steve’s face goes blank and he suddenly he’s a dynamo, pulling all sorts of guitar heroics. We go over well with Hal, Joanne and Massimo.

We pose for pictures with the CFNY crew. It’s my first time meeting them and Joanne is a cute pixie of a girl. Glenn makes a beeline for her and stands right beside her as we get our photos taken.

On the ride home we warn Glenn to stay away from Joanne.

Marvelous Beauhunks at the Marquee Club
(Photo—Adam Graham Collection)

A LETTER FROM CFNY

Tuesday, April 16, 1991

Holy Smokes!

Your entry has been selected as a semi-finalist in this year's 1991 Modern Music Search. We had an enormous amount of talent to choose from so it wasn't an easy decision. Honest!

The playback of all 50 finalists will begin April 22nd, 1991. The times are as follows:

12:53 a.m.
11:53 a.m.
3:53 p.m.

Be sure to listen for your entry, and . . . beginning June 1st, playback of the champions (all ten) will begin. Same time, same station.

Boffo!

Hal Harbour,

Director of Canadian Music Development

cfny FM 102 MODERN ROCK

April 16, 1991

STEVE WRIGHT
THE MARVELOUS BEAUHUNKS
782 RITSON RD. S. #2
OSHAWA, ONTARIO
L1H 5L1

Holy Smokes!

Your entry has been selected as a semi-finalist in this year's 1991 Modern Music Search. We had an enormous amount of talent to choose from so it wasn't an easy decision. Honest!

The playback of all 50 finalists will begin April 22, 1991. The times are as follows:

12:53 a.m.
11:53 a.m.
3:53 p.m.

Be sure to listen for your entry, and... beginning June 1st, playback of the champions (all ten) will begin. Same time, same station.

Boffo!

Hal Harbour,
Director Of Canadian Music Development

HH/fk

Hal.

83 Kennedy Rd. South, Brampton, Ontario L6W 3P3 (416) 453-7452 Fax: 453-7711
Sales Office: 1 Yonge Street, 25th Floor, Toronto, Ontario M5E 1G1 (416) 365-2153 Fax: 960-5412

KEY Radio Limited

A Subsidiary of Maclean Hunter

(Letter—Stephen Wright Collection)

Tuesday, April 23, 1991

Johnny Thunders died today.

That's a drag.

Wednesday, April 24, 1991

Our bathtub is one of those old claw-foot numbers with no shower.

Some days, I like to soak in a hot tub and read comic books.

Spider-man, Wolverine, X-Men, the Punisher.

I'm listening to the top 50 semi-finalists on CFNY.

We're already on the disc.

TRENT MUSIC FESTIVAL, PETERBOROUGH

Friday, April 26, 1991 (11 a.m.-7 p.m.)

North Parking Lot CC—No Drugs or Alcohol allowed

Childcare & Littlefolks Area, Craft & Food Area (live clean—lug-a-mug)

Bands:

Alchemy
Badass Newgrass
Mike Knight & Glen Martin
Kevin Bowers
John Campbell
Conrad Blues
The Cynical Fish
Doug Droul
Dan Fewings & Chris Lakerdas
Group Soul
Hogwash
Iggy Iguana & the Salamander Kings
Ken, Kim, John & Ken
Barry Labrick & Dave Dolejsi
The Leisure Bros.

Marvelous Beauhunks

Mike Martyn
Mary-Clare & Jay

Minglewood
Nutty Fingers
Tim O'Dacre
Marx for Narx
Steve & Stu
Tin Pan Alley
Token Folk
Uptown Rhythm
The Wandering Menstrals
The Whatever Faction

(Flyer—Derek Supryka Collection)

TRENT MUSIC FESTIVAL (THE NIGHT BEFORE)

Thursday, April 25, 1991

Road trip.

Peterborough.

We're playing what used to be called "Bacchus", the end-of-the-year blowout at Trent University.

This year they're calling it the "Trent University Music Festival." It's supposed to the same idea but without the sex, drugs and alcohol. This new "political correctness" is fucking gay. There's nowhere on Earth more politically correct than Trent University.

It's still a good opportunity for us to tap into the college market. Twenty-eight bands playing on a flat-bed truck, looking into a field. To get on the bill we have to have one registered Trent student in the band. This weekend, our friend James will be our token maraca player.

Tonight, we're crashing on various floors at Jimmy's residence.

But first we're on the piss.

TRENT MUSIC FESTIVAL (THE MORNING BEFORE THE SHOW)

Friday, April 26, 1991

My head hurts.

Last night, Derek threw up under a table and tried to hide it. We were kicked out of the pub.

Jimmy tells us that the bathrooms are co-ed. All I see in the shower is Adam's naked ass and I'm disappointed.

We still don't know where Glenn ended up for the night.

Steve's meeting Damyana, so we're all going our separate ways until show-time.

I need something greasy for my hangover.

TRENT MUSIC FESTIVAL (JUST BEFORE THE SHOW)

Friday, April 26, 1991

Where the fuck is he?

We're on next and there's no sign of Steve.

Adam, Derek, and I are waiting at the side of the stage and we're getting panicky. Glenn's out front, winking at the lead singer of the Wandering Menstrals. Christ, doesn't he ever give it a rest?

I swear if Steve's late, I'm out of here. I'll quit this fucking band.

Oh.

Here he comes.

TRENT MUSIC FESTIVAL (THE SHOW)

Friday, April 26, 1991

"This song's for Johnny Thunders who died the other day. It's called *City Asleep*. We'll miss you Johnny."

Golf claps cut the silence. By the looks of the granola-hippies who showed up for this clambake, nobody knows who the fuck Johnny Thunders is.

But Glenn's not finished yet.

"Hey—you cops back there. Are you getting enough donuts?"

Adam and I share a look. That probably wasn't a smart thing to say.

I count us in, hit my snare on the four, and my drum stick breaks in half. There's no time to switch it for a new one so I do the best I can. Then, the beater comes off my kick pedal so there's no kick drum either. Later, I'm told that it looked like I was playing with my bare hand so I let people think that. All things considered, we were well received.

We pack up and hit the one-fifteen home.

Glenn drops acid and he and Cathy drive home with some of his friends.

Way to go rock star.

Glenn Goodman, Adam Graham at the Trent Music Festival (Photo—Adam Graham Collection)

Saturday, April 27, 1991

My 24th birthday.

The Barenaked Ladies are sold-out at the El Mocambo tonight.

Bastards.

.s

ANA 3AM—THE SPECTRUM

dnesday, May 8, 1991

We've got so much good stuff going on that I'm almost not disappointed that we didn't get the Havana 3AM gig.

They're touring with a rockabilly act from the States called Flat Duo Jets.

It would've been cool though.

STRATENGERS, TORONTO—w/ The Life

Wednesday, May 15, 1991

We've gone from Sunday night to Wednesday night in just over a month. We're trailing the accursed Barenaked Ladies who were here this past Saturday. Although we're not bringing in huge numbers, we're starting to draw people in.

I listened to the cassette from the board mix and we're dropping *I'm Crying* by the Animals. We've never worked out a proper arrangement for the backing vocals and it's just a bunch of off-key caterwauling.

Eric Burdon would be spinning in his grave.

If he were dead.

SOUND OF MUSIC FESTIVAL, BURLINGTON—w/ Monday Nuns

Thursday, May 30, 1991

Through Joanne at CFNY, Derek was called by a local promoter named Rocky. Rocky's looking for a band to do a two-night stand in Burlington, hotel included.

The first night is for the Sound of Music Festival, at the Pig and Whistle. The second night is opening for BMG recording artists, the Corndogs, at the Pig's Ear.

The Pig's Ear is the same address as the Pig and Whistle. I have no idea what the difference is. Rocky explained it to Derek but Derek doesn't get it either.

We'll leave right after work on Thursday to play the first gig and come back home after the second gig on Friday. That way I can still work Saturday morning.

Thursday will be Adam's last day of being employed. He's been laid-off.

That's not a bad way to celebrate—signing on for U.I.C. and playing in a band.

SOUND OF MUSIC FESTIVAL, BURLINGTON—w/ Monday Nuns

Thursday, May 30, 1991

Not much of a festival. There's nobody here.

Of the other bands, the only one that we click with is a trio from Hamilton, called the Monday Nuns. They're nice guys named Gene and Mike, and a third whose name I didn't catch.

During our set, the sound man tells Derek that we need to work on our vocals. He also calls us out when we try to pass *Debbie Jones* off as one of our own songs.

For the last while we've been telling Adam not to sing into the mike, because he sounds terrible. He insists on doing it anyway. As we play our last song, *Nice Legs (Shame About Her Face)* by the Monks, Adam's still chirping in with his bleating background vocals.

During the last line of the song, Steve and Glenn are supposed to repeat "Nice Legs, Shame About Her Face" two times, to end it. When it was time for their first line, they sang it together and Adam chimed in. When it was time to sing the line for the second time, Steve and Glenn looked at each other and sang nothing.

As predicted, Adam went right up to the mike, and honked out "Nice Legs, Shame About Her Face" all by himself, sounding like a goose in flight. His face went red.

As we left the stage, Adam was in a rage. "If you guys ever pull another stunt like that again, I'm putting down my bass and walking off!"

Laughing in his face, Steve said, "Go ahead."

WHAT THE HELL IS GOING ON?

CFMU FM 93.3

presents

FRI MAY 31

THE CORNDOGS

at

THE PIG'S EAR

with special guests

MARVELOUS BOHUNKS

Latent RECORDINGS
DISTRIBUTED BY BMG MUSIC CANADA INC
MUSIQUE BMG DU CANADA INC

COVER $3.

THE PIG'S EAR, BURLINGTON (MORNING)—w/ The Corndogs

Friday, May 31, 1991

Last night was fun.

Rocky bought us a case of beer and a pizza after the show. He was disappointed when we didn't want to stay up all night and party with him. Steve, Adam, and I had worked all day and by midnight we were ready for sleep.

Glenn was up for it and he disappeared. Around five, he rolled back into the room. They'd found him sleeping on a bench outside. The hotel threatened to kick us all out.

By 10 a.m., housekeeping ordered us to vacate the room. We were only comped one night and now we have to leave. We're stranded in Burlington with nowhere to go until show time. We debate going back to seven-eighty-two and returning for the gig, but there's a radio interview at two o'clock with the Corndogs at McMaster University.

We get breakfast and check out the local sites before settling in on the hotel lawn for the rest of the day. As we lay around on the grass, Glenn springs up, crushes my Ray Bans, and points at the lake shouting, "I'm sailing, I'm sailing!" I don't know what the fuck he's talking about but I'm heartbroken over losing my prized specs.

When the Corndogs arrive, it's in a beaten-up, brown GMC van. These guys are the real deal. As we talk with their drummer and the singer, a prone figure stirs on the floor in the back of the van. "That's my brother Lionel," says the drummer. "He's the bass player."

When the drummer asks me if I smoke, I tell him I do, but that I'm out of cigarettes. He laughs and walks away with the singer.

Adam tells me that he was asking me if I smoked pot.

I had no idea.

THE PIG'S EAR, BURLINGTON (AFTERNOON)—w/ The Corndogs

Friday, May 31, 1991

At interview time, the Corndogs suggest that we drive with them in their van. These guys are in their 30s and have a couple of major label albums out. They've got the miles on their faces to prove it.

Tucked away with their gear is a canvas backdrop that says "The Corndogs." Scrawled all over it, are punters' signatures from every show they've done. We think that's really cool and we file the idea away for later.

Today is Steve's turn to threaten to quit the band. Derek only wanted two of us to go to the interview and he thought it should be Glenn and me. Steve was pissed off and wouldn't talk to anybody. He just walked around with his fists balled up.

Now all five of us from the MBH camp are crammed into the studio with the deejay and two of the Corndogs. When the Corndogs are asked a question, they speak one at a time and sound like professionals. When the Marvelous Beauhunks are asked a question, all five of us talk at the same time and we sound like idiots.

The Corndogs drop us back at the hotel, and we resume our waiting on the lawn. I'd do anything for a pillow and a book. The tedium's broken when Joanne shows up with the hot-off-the-presses, CFNY Modern Music CD. She tells us to get registered with SOCAN in order to get paid for the airtime CFNY's giving us.

We're in heavy rotation.

As a bonus, we're all given black "Modern Music Search" tee-shirts and suddenly the waiting seems worth it.

Our *esprit de corps* is cut short when the girlfriends show up to "surprise us." I don't know if Steve and Glenn planned for this, but I'm disappointed.

Nothing kills an "all lads together" vibe faster than the arrival of wives and girlfriends.

(Photo—Trish Mennell)

THE PIG'S EAR, BURLINGTON (SHOWTIME)—w/ The Corndogs

Friday, May 31, 1991

What a waste of a night. There's only two people here that aren't somehow attached to one of the bands.

That's a shame, because I dig the Corndogs. We have to wait until they're done playing before we can go home. It wouldn't be cool to leave earlier—then the room would be completely empty.

They deserve better than that.

Rocky's gotta be taking a bath on this.

REHEARSAL

Tuesday, June 4, 1991

Glenn's been keeping secrets from us.

He's quite the talent with his mum's sewing machine. Tonight, he's shown up to practice with two of her white bed sheets sewn together, complete with little ties along the top to hang it up with. Also in his arsenal are two cans of spray paint—black and orange.

As resident artist of the group, it falls to me to spray the band's logo on our new backdrop.

The four of us stand in front of seven-eighty-two and admire the finished product. Now all we need to do is fill it up with signatures like the Corndogs did.

We leave it on the lawn to dry while we go inside to rehearse.

EAST SHORE COMMUNITY CENTRE, PICKERING w/ hHead, The Mindset, Heebee Gee

Sunday, June 9, 1991

Derek booked us to play an all-ages show at a coffee-house in Pickering. We aren't sure what to make of that. Playing in front of people drinking coffee on a Sunday afternoon sounds weird.

When we get there, it isn't a coffee-house at all. It's the East Shore Community Centre and it's full of kids and grandparents.

The Mindset are here too. The band playing before us are called "hHead" . . . with two h's. We're the only band with a song on the radio and we think this gig is beneath us. Derek thinks we're being arrogant.

It's hot as hell and the acoustics are bad. Glenn sings off key for most of the show, but no one notices anything until he uses the "F-word" in front of the five-year-olds.

As a basketball bounces past me, I lose interest in the whole . . .

SET LIST

Sunday, June 9, 1991

Happy Together—the Jam
City Asleep—Marvelous Beauhunks
We Gotta Get Outta This Place—the Animals
Give, Give, Give Me More, More, More—the Wonderstuff
Little Bitch—the Specials
Pictures and Tears—Marvelous Beauhunks
Nice Legs (Shame About Her Face)—the Monks
Kickin' Around—Marvelous Beauhunks
Pressure Drop—the Clash
Fantasy Merry-Go-Round—Marvelous Beauhunks
Debbie Jones—Squire

Monday, June 10, 1991

Fantasy Merry-Go-Round is No. 54 on the CFNY charts.

Thursday, June 13, 1991

My friend Deana and I are at Kingswood to see Elvis Costello.

The weather's taken a surprising turn as the sun goes down and it's cold and windy. We're caught unprepared in our shorts and tee-shirts. The best we can do is huddle together and wait it out.

Up first are the Replacements and they're typically shambolic. They're doing the same shtick as the last time I saw them. False starts and stops, drunk, out of time. I don't get what the big deal is with these guys. Earlier, Tommy Stinson wandered through the crowd wearing a pale blue tuxedo jacket.

CFNY's presenting the concert and they're making a big deal out of the Barenaked Ladies being in the audience. I hate those guys. I want to shout out that I'm here too and that I'm equally famous. But it's too windy and we're too far back on the lawn. Nobody would hear me.

When E.C. hits the stage, he's fat, bearded, and ponytailed.

This isn't any Elvis Costello that I wanna see.

Who the fuck IS THIS pudgy bastard?

THE WHITE ROOM

Saturday, June 15, 1991

We're tackling Glenn's Nana's song, *Pictures and Tears.*

To get a decent sound out of my drums, I'm down a small fortune. I've replaced every head, top to bottom. Ten drum-heads in total.

But despite my significant investment and several hours of tuning and re-tuning, my drums still sound like Tupperware. The problem is the shells. They're made from a composite material and they don't record like real wood does. There's nothing more we can do.

With everyone's levels set, we capture the bed tracks by the third take. The arrangement for *Pictures and Tears* is our most sophisticated to date. Adam's playing a 1972 American-made, Fender Jazz bass now. This is really filling out the bottom end. Steve's trying a lot of new sounds in the studio and, by far, the most interesting is a backwards guitar melody in the middle eight.

To make the backwards effect, Scotty took the tape out of the TASCAM recorder, flipped it over and hit "Play." Everything we'd recorded up until that point, came through the speakers in reverse and Steve played along to it. When he was done, Scotty flipped the tape back the right way and what came out was "instant Beatles."

When Steve finishes the rest of his guitar tracks, we'll quit and do the vocals in the morning.

THE WHITE ROOM

Sunday, June 16, 1991

Working a half-day. Tonight is the Modern Music CD release at the Copa.

As a bonus band on the disc, we're not eligible to play the show or to receive any prizes. Instead, we've been getting the most airplay out of any group. That's prize enough for me. I can't listen to CFNY without hearing our song every couple of hours.

I'm passing on tonight's festivities though. I'm tired. Scotty's using my ticket instead.

After we finish the vocals, they'll head downtown and I'll head home for Sunday night TV.

(Photo—Trish Mennell)

CFNY MODERN MUSIC SHOWCASE
—the Copa, Toronto

Sunday June 16, 1991

Doors open at 7:00 PM—Legal Age 19 Required

I.C.E.
SING ALONG WITH TONTO
SKAFACE
DIGITAL POODLE
PRAY FOR RAIN
DIGIT
THE FRINGE

THE WHITE ROOM

Monday, June 17, 1991

Once we're done mixing *Pictures and Tears*, Glenn and Derek are taking it straight to CFNY.

Six months ago, we were playing Pizza Pino's and now we have the No. 37 song on the charts of the coolest radio station in Canada. *Fantasy Merry-Go-Round* has already jumped 17 positions since last week.

That puts us seven spots away from breaking the Top 30.

I wonder if we're really as good as people are making us out to be. The other guys don't seem to be questioning it, and even Scotty's a believer now.

Our goal is to make it at least past No. 15 on the charts. That's where the Barenaked Ladies peaked with their novelty song *Be My Yoko Ono*, last year.

Considering that the top three songs on the charts this week are Crash Test Dummies (*Superman's Song*), Julian Cope (*Beautiful Love*) and Elvis Costello (*The Other Side of Summer*), we may actually have a chance at breaking the Top 10.

Monday, June 24, 1991

We're up 13 spots and sitting at No. 24.

Fantasy Merry-Go-Round has broken the Top 30.

People are telling me they're hearing *Pictures and Tears* on the air as well.

Too much.

CFNY CANADA DAY FESTIVAL—MOLSON PARK, BARRIE

Monday, July 1, 1991

Blue Rodeo
Violent Femmes
Dream Warriors
Crash Test Dummies
Skydiggers
Spirit of the West
Teenage Head
Bootsauce
King Apparatus
Skaface

CFNY CANADA DAY FESTIVAL—MOLSON PARK, BARRIE

Monday, July 1, 1991

Glenn is using his newfound celebrity status for good.

He and Davy went to Molson Park for CFNY's Canada Day Festival. They didn't have tickets and they tried to jump the fence. When they heard someone yelling at them, they were about to leg it.

Then they realized it was Hal Harbour.

"Glenn. Hey, Glenn. Over here!"

He gave them backstage passes.

Davy ended up dancing on stage with the Violent Femmes.

Goodman's got a horseshoe up his arse.

STRATENGERS, TORONTO—w/ Smalltown Preachers

Thursday, July 4, 1991

Introduction

Glenn:
"We're the Marvelous Beauhunks from Oshawa. For those of you who don't know who we are, or where Oshawa is, you don't wanna know . . . . Kick it!"

1. TYNL

2. Pressure Drop

Steve Closs:
"Put on your red shoes and dance the blues . . . (Steve Wright is fixing kick pedal) . . . let's guess that drum problem tonight."

Steve Wright:
"You don't wanna know my problems . . .

"I'd like to take this opportunity to say hello to the three healthy looking young women in the front row whom I didn't get a chance to talk to earlier this evening. Hello girls."

Glenn:
Laughs . . .

3. Happy Together

Skinheads yelling:
"In the City!"

4. My Mind Goes Round in Circles

Glenn:
"Gonna take you back to the '60s."

5. Heart Full of Soul

Glenn:
"K! We're gonna slow it down jest a li'l bit . . . (in a southern drawl)

OK! This next song is one of our many recorded songs . . . how many? Too numerous to mention . . . it's called Dare to Dream."

6. Dare to Dream

7. Give Me More

Steve Wright:
"Thank you ever so much. There's something wrong with the dance floor tonight, Glenn."

Skinhead with Brit accent repeatedly shouting:
"In the Cityyyyy."

Glenn:
"OK! The next number we're gonna do has got the word "City" in it. That should shut you up for a few minutes. This is called City Asleep."

8. City Asleep

Skinhead with Brit accent repeatedly shouting:
"In the Cityyyyy."

Steve Wright:
"I see we're being visited by the sarcastic clap family tonight."

Glenn:
"You people ever have too much time on your hands?"

Skinhead with Brit accent repeatedly shouting:
"In the Cityyyyy."

Glenn:
"The next song we're gonna do is called Kickin' Around."

British accented groans in the background

Skinhead with Brit accent repeatedly shouting:
"In the Cityyyyy."

9. Kickin' Around

Skinhead with Brit accent shouting:
"Oi, oi, oi, oi, oi, oi, oi . . ."

Glenn:
"These guys are hounding us . . . is there any security here?"

Steve Wright:
"Nope. Just a lot of insecurity."

Glenn:
"This next song is about our home town Oshawa."

Skinhead with Brit accent repeatedly shouting:
"In the Cityyyyy."

Glenn:
"This next song is called We Gotta Get Outta This Place."

10. We Gotta Get Out of This Place

Glenn:
"This next song is Pictures and Tears."

11. Pictures and Tears

Skinhead with Brit accent shouting:
"Pretty Vayyy-cunnnt."

Glenn:
"This is Nice Legs."

12. Nice Legs (Shame About Her Face)

Skinhead with Brit accent shouting:
"In the facking Cit-eeeee."

13. Little Bitch

Glenn:
"Fuck. That one was for the fucking garbage can. OK! On with the show . . . on with the show."

Skinhead with Brit accent shouting:
"Pretty Vayyy-cunnnt."

Glenn:
"This is called Fantasy Merry-Go-Round. We're gonna tease you a little bit first."

14. Fantasy Merry-Go-Round

Skinhead with Brit accent shouting:
"Pretty Vayyy-cunnnt."

Glenn:
"OK! This next song we're gonna do . . . (Sound man says that there's no next song) . . . what is that it? A short one. A quick short one just to shut these people up."

Steve Closs:
"This is a song about our lives and our fans."

Glenn:
"We swore we'd never do this . . ."

15. Pretty Vacant

Skinhead gets on stage and counts:
"Eins, zwei, drei, vier . . ."

It's time to get the fuck out of here.

Stephen Closs at Stratengers
(Photo—Adam Graham Collection)

Monday, July 8, 1991

We're No. 16.

I'm listening to CFNY in my car when *Fantasy Merry-Go-Round* comes on.

I crank the volume.

Steve's driving north on Ritson Road. We pass each other in a frenzy, both pointing at our radios, music blaring.

We're bouncing up and down in our seats, laughing.

It doesn't get better than this.

Tuesday, July 9, 1991

Derek's doing some schmoozing at CFNY. EMF are touring their single *Unbelievable* and promoting their gig at the Concert Hall. *Fantasy Merry-Go-Round* is the song that plays before their studio interview begins.

Derek tells the EMF guys that he's our manager. They tell Derek that they like our song.

What else are they going to say?

They're English.

TAKING IT ONE (BEAU) HUNK AT A TIME

Oshawa This Week, Wednesday, July 10, 1991
By John Duarte

You can't really blame Oshawa's latest music sensations, the Marvelous Beauhunks, for being a little awed by what's going on around them.

The Oshawa foursome exploded on the music scene this year after alternative rock radio station CFNY-FM picked the band to be on its Modern Rock compilation album.

"That alone has given the band so much credibility," says Beauhunk Glenn Goodman, the band's lead singer. "It's definitely given us a boost."

. . .

" . . . But, for now, the Marvelous Beauhunks are just enjoying what is happening.

"Anytime anyone comes up to us and recognizes us, it's a great feeling," says Goodman.

Graham, however, best sums up the year the Marvelous Beauhunks have had. "We jumped right into the Toronto market. We were very lucky."

. . .

Derek caught us by surprise when he said the Oshawa This Week wanted to send someone over to interview us for a feature in the entertainment section.

We laughed about it. Is this for real?

Are we really an overnight sensation?

Or is it really just a slow news day in Oshawa?

Thursday, July 11, 1991

I'm an official, bona fide member of SOCAN.

Time to get paid for all that *Fantasy Merry-Go-Round* airplay.

Hahaha . . .

Suckers.

THE MARQUEE, TORONTO—w/ The Monday Nuns

Thursday, July 11, 1991

We've brought the Monday Nuns from Hamilton to play with us. Also on the roster is Heebee Gee. Between the three bands, there should've been a bigger crowd.

For every "Marvelous Beauhunks" ticket that came through the door, we're paid a dollar.

My take for the night is twenty cents.

And that's still better than the Monday Nuns did.

It's only rock and roll and I like it.

But honestly, I'd like it even more if I was able to eat it.

Friday, July 12, 1991

Derek called with some exciting news.

We're headlining UltraSound, on August 22, with the Coles and the Smalltown Preachers. CFNY is sponsoring the show as part of their Discovery Mobile Music series, which means that we'll be recorded from a mobile studio and broadcast later on CFNY.

UltraSound is the hottest club in Toronto and where all the up-and-comers play: Lowest of the Low, the Waltons, Barenaked Ladies, the Rheostatics, etc.

This is the type of showcase that brings out the record companies so this could be a very big break for us.

We'd better not fuck it up.

Saturday, July 13, 1991

Maria kissed me in the parking lot.

"I'll be back in a month," she said. "You better call me."

I promised that I would and then left for home.

Earlier that day I'd been a groomsman for my old friend Mike. Mike and I had fallen out of touch over the last three years and I'd been surprised when he asked me to stand up for him on his big day. Later, when his new sister-in-law implied that I'd been included merely to round out the wedding party, it began to make sense.

But the day hadn't been a total waste. Maria was there. She was a friend of the new sister-in-law and we'd met a few times before at the Ozone. Despite our mutual attraction, she'd been warned about me. That made me even more interested.

I liked her long black hair and big hoop earrings. She looked like an Italian Justine Bateman but with more going on upstairs than Mallory Keaton. Maria was smart, and she was about to embark on a new career as an elementary school teacher.

In the morning, she was leaving for Vancouver, driving someone's car across Canada with the new sister-in-law.

She'll be back in a month.

I can hardly wait.

Monday, July 15, 1991

We've lost ground on the CFNY charts. Looks like No. 16 is as high as we're going to make it. That's pretty phenomenal, but still . . . .

We didn't beat the Barenaked Ladies.

LEE'S PALACE, TORONTO—w/ the Life, Surrender Dorothy

Saturday, July 20, 1991

Lee's Palace.

This is pure fantasy-fulfillment. I've wanted to be on this stage ever since I saw the Purple Toads, UIC, and the Dik Van Dykes play here in the mid-'80s.

I saw Breeding Ground here too. I thought they were a pretty big band until their singer was serving me drinks at the Silver Crown one night. That was an eye-opener.

The Life really have it figured out when it comes to putting on a show. They've chartered a bus to ship their fans in from Durham Region and the room is packed tight with the hottest girls. Every table and flat surface is littered with "Life Newsletters" that detail the band's history and upcoming shows. These guys are great at creating their own spin. We'll be stealing these ideas for our UltraSound gig.

The sound system at Lee's is fantastic. Despite what happened at the Pig's Ear in Burlington, Adam is still honking away into the mike. What he doesn't know is that Steve talked to the soundman before the show. Adam's vocals are coming through the stage monitors but not the house speakers. Nobody can hear him. It's weird that he's got such a bug up his arse about singing. I'm pretty sure that if people told me I sounded like a cunt, I'd just stop doing it.

Despite Adam's wailing into a silent mike, we're going over well. Glenn jumps from the stage and dances in the crowd while Steve leaps around like Paul Weller. My friend Lori wiggles out of her bra and hurls it at me on stage.

When Steve makes the obligatory "you've heard this on CFNY" introduction to *Fantasy Merry-Go-Round*, I play my big, fuck-off drum roll.

The Marvelous Beauhunk star is in full ascension.

Glenn Goodman, Stephen Closs at Lee's Palace
(Photo—Sue Newhouses)

LEE'S PALACE, TORONTO—w/ the Life, Surrender Dorothy

Saturday, July 20, 1991

Set List:

TYNL—Marvelous Beauhunks
Pressure Drop—the Clash
Happy Together—the Jam
Kickin' Around—Marvelous Beauhunks
Give Me More—Wonderstuff
City Asleep—Marvelous Beauhunks
Pictures and Tears—Marvelous Beauhunks
Nice Legs (Shame About Her Face)—the Monks
Little Bitch—the Specials
Fantasy Merry-Go-Round—Marvelous Beauhunks
Debbie Jones—Squire

LOCAL BAND SET FOR TORONTO GIG

The Oshawa Times, Saturday, July 20, 1991

Four South Oshawa musicians, with a song on the CFNY music chart, will be playing Toronto this summer.

The Marvelous Beauhunks are playing the UltraSound Show Bar on August 22.

Made up of Steve Wright, Glenn Goodman, Steve Closs, and Adam Graham, the Beauhunks are also planning the release of an album this fall. They've already produced four songs; Fantasy Merry-Go-Round, Pictures and Tears, Dare to Dream and TYNL.

Last month, Fantasy Merry-Go-Round was released on the 1991 Modern Music Search, got airplay on radio station CFNY and made it to the charts. The band has also played at clubs in and around the Toronto area since it formed in 1990.

The band writes its own material and the sound has a distinctive British flavor to it. Reminiscent of the British invasion of the 60s, band-members say that they are influenced in their music by bands such as the Yardbirds, the Clash, the Beatles and the Jam.

Wright performs drums and vocals and writes lyrics. Goodman handles vocals and writes lyrics. Closs, a founding member, is the bandleader and his pop hooks are the basis for the band's compositions. He plays guitars and does vocals. Graham handles vocals and bass guitar and works on the lyrics.

CORKTOWN TAVERN, HAMILTON—w/ Monday Nuns, Cockleshell Heroes

Thursday, July 25, 1991

The Monday Nuns have invited us to play a show on their home turf of Hamilton.

As before, there's no one here. Just us, the Monday Nuns and the other band, the Cockleshell Heroes.

It turns out that Steve and the guitar-player from the Cockleshell Heroes know each other from various mod/ska events in Toronto.

Corktown's a good room, but it was a long drive for a lame night.

ULTRASOUND, TORONTO—w/ Trouble with Jan

Monday, July 29, 1991

Besides us, one of the only bands from Oshawa making any real Queen Street noise is Trouble With Jan.

There's a few social connections between us, and they also record at Scotty's. It's only been a matter of time before our paths crossed.

They're doing a month of Mondays at UltraSound and they asked us to open for them on the first night of their residency. It was a good opportunity for us to get a feel for the stage before we do our live recording here on the 22nd.

Our set was probably the tightest we've played to date. During the guitar break in *Little Bitch,* I flipped my trilby over to Steve. He placed it on his head for a second and then flipped it over to Glenn.

Glenn popped it on, jumped on the dance floor, and performed a "Suggs-from-Madness-meets-Chuck-Berry-duck-walk." He was on fire. I don't think Trouble With Jan were happy to follow that.

Yvonne, UltraSound's manager and talent-booker, loved us.

She said we reminded her of being back home in England.

We're gold.

THE SILVER DOLLAR, TORONTO—w/ Scam Artists and Heebee Gee

Friday, August 2, 1991

The Silver Dollar's a fun place to play. There's a bathtub under the stage, a strip club downstairs, and one of the last cigarette machines in Toronto.

Here's the best moment of the night:

We're on stage doing our thing. There's a drunken girl dancing on the bar, throwing ice cubes at us. All of a sudden Glenn drops to his knees like a sack of wet cement and he's pawing frantically at his groin.

The mighty Gooders, brought down by a dancing girl with an ice cube.

Outstanding.

On a separate note, I've learned that six pints of 10% beer will impede your sexual performance.

Well, my sexual performance anyway.

Glenn Goodman about to be taken down at the Silver Dollar
(Photo—April Benegbi)

THE WHITE ROOM

Saturday (Morning), August 10, 1991

The plan is to finish up enough material for a six-song EP.

We'll release it on cassette, get some product out there, then work on a full-length CD for release early next year.

With three in the can (*Fantasy Merry-Go-Round*, *Dare to Dream*, and *Pictures and Tears*), we'll knock off *City Asleep* and *Kickin' Around* in short order. The fact that Glenn has a summer cold isn't enough of a deterrent to reschedule today's session.

As an added bonus, the keyboard player from the Smalltown Preachers has agreed to record Hammond B3 organ and harmonica on *TYNL*.

This means Adam has one last chance at getting the bass right.

He'd better fucking nail it.

THE WHITE ROOM

Saturday (Afternoon), August 10, 1991

We're listening to the playbacks for *TYNL*.

"Hey! Who's that playing bass?" Adam asks, walking into the room.

"Don't you recognize your own playing?" replies Steve, "That's you."

While the bed tracks for *City Asleep* and *Kickin' Around* went down quickly, Adam once again fumbled the bassline for *TYNL*. After two hours, we took a break and Adam went out to clear his head.

Once Adam was gone, Steve asked the Preacher's keyboard player if he could do a Doors-style bassline with his left hand while he was recording his B3 parts with his right hand.

"Sure," he said.

Five minutes later, *TYNL* was finished.

Now that Steve's trying to pass this off as Adam's own playing, Adam is pissed-off and indignant.

"That's not me," Adam says, storming out of the room. "I'm not a fucking idiot, you know."

Glenn and I are rolling on the floor laughing.

Scotty's shaking his head in disgust.

Of the six songs we've recorded for this EP, Adam says that *TYNL* is the one that he likes the least.

THE WHITE ROOM

Monday, August 12, 1991

After work tonight, we went over to Scotty's to mix *City Asleep.*

I really like the way this one turned out.

At the last minute, Steve had improvised a neat, melodic guitar-line to put over it. The song really came to life after that.

So far no one has called me out on the Mick Fleetwood-type stutters that I do between the snare and cymbal shots.

It's probably for the best that I don't point it out.

THE WHITE ROOM

Wednesday, August 14, 1991

Kickin' Around is in the can.

Once *TYNL* is properly mixed, we'll have our EP.

It's fitting that we release the first songs we wrote together as one recording.

THE WHITE ROOM

Friday, August 16, 1991

TYNL is FINALLY done.

I'm actually a little disappointed in the mix though. The keyboard bassline doesn't have the same bottom-end that a real bass does. It's a little light-weight.

Even so, it's still better than what Adam was playing.

Steve has this idea that he wants to record three of his mother's music boxes, playing out of synch with each other. This will be the intro to *Fantasy Merry-Go-Round* as the first song on the EP.

OSHAWA'S BEAUHUNKS HEADLINE AT ULTRASOUND

Oshawa/Whitby This Week, Sunday Edition, Sunday, August 18, 1991

Oshawa's own Marvelous Beauhunks will play at Ultrasound, in Toronto, on Thursday night. Admission to the show costs $3.

THE WHITE ROOM

Tuesday, August 19, 1991

We're skipping rehearsal tonight in order to record Steve's mum's music boxes. We'll also sequence the songs for the EP.

Scotty's got the music boxes set up and miked on Steve's guitar case in the live room. They're playing out of time with one another. With reverb and delay on them, they sound freaky and ethereal. Like a creepy carnival.

The running order of the cassette will be:

Side One—*Fantasy Merry-Go-Round / Dare to Dream / City Asleep*

Side Two—*Pictures and Tears / Kickin' Around / TYNL*

Now, all we need to do is come up with the money to have it manufactured. And to decide on a cover and title.

A talented local artist, Wolfgang Mueller, has offered to paint the cover art for free. This is a major coup and we're all excited about it. At least most of us are.

Predictably, Steve's being obstinate. He wants his brother to design the cover. He's also vetoed every suggestion we've made for the title, even though doesn't have any suggestions of his own.

This is becoming a frustrating pattern. Every time the rest of us are in agreement on something, Steve automatically takes a contrary position. Most times he doesn't have any reason other than he's got us over a barrel.

No Steve—no band.

Sadly, he's not wrong.

Tuesday, August 20, 1991

Adam and I went downtown to poster Queen Street for the big UltraSound show.

We've got our flyers and a couple of demo tapes with press kits. We want to book gigs at the Rivoli and the Horseshoe. Especially the Horseshoe.

The Horseshoe, UltraSound and X-Ray's are all under the same management. Yvonne from UltraSound already likes us, so we should have a good shot at getting into the Horseshoe.

Adam and I ask the bartender who we should speak to. We're directed to a back office. Our eyes adjust to the dim lighting. We see Jabba the Hutt sprawled across the couch. No, it's not Jabba the Hutt. It's the main man himself, X-Ray.

As Adam begins his pitch, X-Ray waves him off with a grunt. "Leave your stuff on the desk."

Our audience with greatness is over.

I'm creeped-out by the experience. Adam's offended that X-Ray hasn't even bothered to stand up to address us.

It doesn't really matter to me.

I have low expectations from a grown man who calls himself "X-Ray".

HUNK-MAIL NEWSLETTER (VOLUME 1, ISSUE 1)

Thursday, August 22, 1991

For those of you unfamiliar with the MARVELOUS BEAUHUNKS, a quick recap:

February, 1990:

The result of a horrible accident, the MARVELOUS BEAUHUNKS are given life in a South Oshawa basement. A quick drawing of straws decides the line-up:

Glenn Goodman—vocals
"Little" Stephen Closs—guitar
Adam Graham—bass
Stephen Wright—drums

The resulting sound can only be described as "Hey! You guys sound like my favourite band!!!"

MARVELOUS BEAUHUNKS appear on the "1991 CFNY Modern Music CD." Much thanks to Joanne, Hal, and everyone else who pulled for us!

MARVELOUS BEAUHUNKS have just finished recordings for their first six song cassette available this fall (remember charitable donations are tax deductable). Tracks include: Fantasy Merry-Go-Round, TYNL, Kickin' Around, Dare to Dream, Pictures and Tears, and City Asleep. Recording was done at White Room, with Scotty McClelland engineering. All tracks were produced by the band. Great job Scotty!

Introducing the brand new line of MARVELOUS BEAUHUNKS casual wear. For a nominal fee, you too can have all four Beauhunks pressed against your chest (not just in t-shirt form either). The band will autograph all shirts providing you are female and wearing it. T-shirt design was done by drummer Steve Wright. Excellent thanks to our merchandising team: Sue, John, and April.

MARVELOUS BEAUHUNKS would like to thank those who love and support us, notably: Damyana, Natasha, Julie, CFNY, our merchandisers, Phil (best MC with a British accent), our mums, Yvonne for the gig, and everyone who came out tonight. You're great!!!

Upcoming gala BEAUHUNK showings:
Niagara House—Friday, August 30 with THE COLES
Marquee Club—Saturday, August 31 with SCAM ARTISTS
Apocalypse Club—Friday, September 13 with SKA FACE
Underdog (Peterborough)—Saturday, September 21

For more information about tickets, bookings, merchandise, call:
(416) 555-3854 (located at the luxurious MARVELOUS BEAUHUNKS building)
(416) 555-1764 (management headquarters)

Or just call to chat. We'd love it. Really.

** Stephen Closs plays Rickenbacker guitars exclusively.*

ULTRASOUND, TORONTO—CFNY Live Recording (PART 1) w/ The Coles, Smalltown Preachers

Thursday, August 22, 1992

My luck is good. I found a place to park on John Street, right across from UltraSound. After feeding the meter, I legged it up the stairs to meet the other guys at the club.

It's a buzzing beehive of nervous activity. The Coles and the Smalltown Preachers are already here, as well as Yvonne and the recording crew. The stakes are high tonight and all three bands are looking for their big break. No one can afford to mess this up.

As the headlining band, we sound check first. It seems to take forever. The sound engineers have to set the levels just so, for when we hit the stage. They'll be mixing us on the fly and there's very little time to make adjustments. They have to lock it down right out of the gate.

I'm uncomfortably tense. This past week has seen my anxiety shoot up to levels that I've never experienced before. Dark circles have set in beneath my ever-widening eyes and my shoulders feel like they're up around my ears.

It's not stage fright, because I never get that. I know that once I'm behind the kit, my job will get done. It's more like a feeling of being out of control. As if everything in my life is riding on this one moment and if it's a cock-up, there'll be no coming back from it. For days all I've been able to think about is what might go wrong. My mind gets stuck on repeat, replaying these scenarios over and over until I can't block out the thoughts. Coffee and cigarettes are all I consume and they only make it worse.

I keep these thoughts to myself. I'm afraid that people will think that there's something wrong with me.

After we finish sound check, there's several hours to kill. Adam, Lisa and I walk down Queen Street looking for dinner. A homeless person startles me and asks for spare change.

My fight or flight response kicks in and I go berserk.

"Get away from me!" I yell, panicking and ready to attack. "Don't touch me! Why don't you get a fucking job and leave me the fuck alone? Get out of here!"

The homeless man backs up, looking at me the way one person looks at another when they unravel right before them.

"Your friend needs some help," he says to Adam.

Adam and Lisa stand there in shock, mouths open.

I walk on ahead, wondering what's been happening to me.

ULTRASOUND, TORONTO—CFNY Live Recording (PART 2) w/ The Coles, Smalltown Preachers

Thursday, August 22, 1992

At eight o'clock, it's time to change from shorts and tee-shirts into something better suited for the stage.

I walk to my car to grab my clothes.

Where's my car?

I look again to make sure this is the parking spot where I left it.

It is.

My first thought is that my car's been stolen. Then I look at the sign posted by the curb.

No parking between 5:00 and 7:00 p.m.

The bastards towed me.

I rifle the phone book and find the number for the nearest police division. They put me in touch with the company that's got the city's towing contract. Yes, they've got a red Chevette there. Come down to Lakeshore Blvd to collect it.

Five minutes later we're in Adam's truck, with Adam laughing hysterically behind the wheel, as he drives me to the impound yard.

Somehow, I'm able to squeeze an additional $150 onto my credit card and they point me in the direction of my car. Under the wiper blades are sixty-dollars in parking tickets.

What else can go wrong?

ULTRASOUND, TORONTO—CFNY Live Recording (PART 3) w/ The Coles, Smalltown Preachers

Thursday, August 22, 1992

Hal Harbour:

"All right I guess we're ready to go here gang. We'd like to thank the Coles and the Smalltown Preachers for really warming up this night at Ultrasound.

I want to thank all the CFNY crew and the Discovery Music Mobile. Reiner Schwarz is here tonight, Joanne Faloona, Karen Fisher, Captain Phil, Rich, Darryl's here from the music department . . .

And let's welcome the band that's too young, too fast, and too cool . . . the MARVELOUS BEAUHUNKS!!!"

Steve riffs the now-familiar, stuttering start-stop intro of *TYNL* and UltraSound heaves.

It's packed pretty tight in here tonight.

CFNY's been announcing on the radio since nine-o'clock that if you weren't already here, you weren't getting in.

Maria's shown up. This is the first time I've seen her since she left for Vancouver a month ago. Although I'm happy that she's come, her presence doesn't create as much excitement for Glenn as the arrival of a certain radio celebrity.

"Rob Reiner's here . . . . ROB REINER'S HERE!!" Glenn shouts to Adam and me.

We're confused. Meathead from *All In the Family* is here? Then it dawns on us. He means Reiner Schwarz, CFNY's Director of Programming & Operations. Adam looks at me and shakes his head.

We're half-way through *TYNL*. Steve nails the solo and we ride into the third verse on a crested wave of adrenalin. Adam's got a cigarette hanging from his mouth "Keef-style" and he's holding his own. People are packed up against the stage, bouncing along in unison to the beat. It's hot, sticky and sweet, but somehow Glenn manages to keep his shirt on. So far, at least.

The first song ends. Steve hits the opening chords to *My Mind Goes Round in Circles*. We're off again.

We play our hearts out. We debut a new original called *Think It Over*. It's our follow-up to *Fantasy Merry-Go-Round* and it goes over well. We're energetic and musically tight. Between songs we're clever, witty, and urbane. I ask the crowd for donations to pay for my towing charge and we're pelted with coins of all denominations. Steve tries to cover his Rickenbacker with his body to avoid it being marked up in the onslaught.

We give away some of our new Marvelous Beauhunks tee-shirts in a draw. The first winner is Steve's ex-girlfriend. Damyana storms off and Adam laughs out loud. We're having the time of our lives.

Between songs, Glenn wipes his brow with his arm. "It's hot as a fuck up here," he says.

Steve, Adam, and I start to vamp an elongated intro to *Fantasy-Merry-Go-Round*. I start my two-bar, thirty-two beat, fuck-off drum roll and the crowd goes wild.

"Yes! You were right!" shouts Glenn into the microphone. The stage is invaded and people are dancing like mad. CFNY's own Captain Phil inadvertently stomps on Steve's foot, but Steve manages to shrug it off and carry on playing.

After letting the crowd chant "*Beauhunks . . . Beauhunks . . . Beauhunks . . .*" for a few minutes, we return to the stage for two encores and leave them wanting more.

Once again, the rent is paid in full.

Things take a slightly sour turn when Derek collects our money. He keeps most of it for the phone bill, leaving us just enough cash for a trip to the hot dog cart.

Damyana starts chirping in Steve's ear and by the look in his eyes, the countdown on Derek has begun.

I don't care because I've just been making out with Maria in the stairwell.

What a night!

Stephen Closs at UltraSound
(Photo—Sue Newhouses)

Stephen Closs, Stephen Wright, Glenn Goodman at UltraSound (Photo—Sue Newhouses)

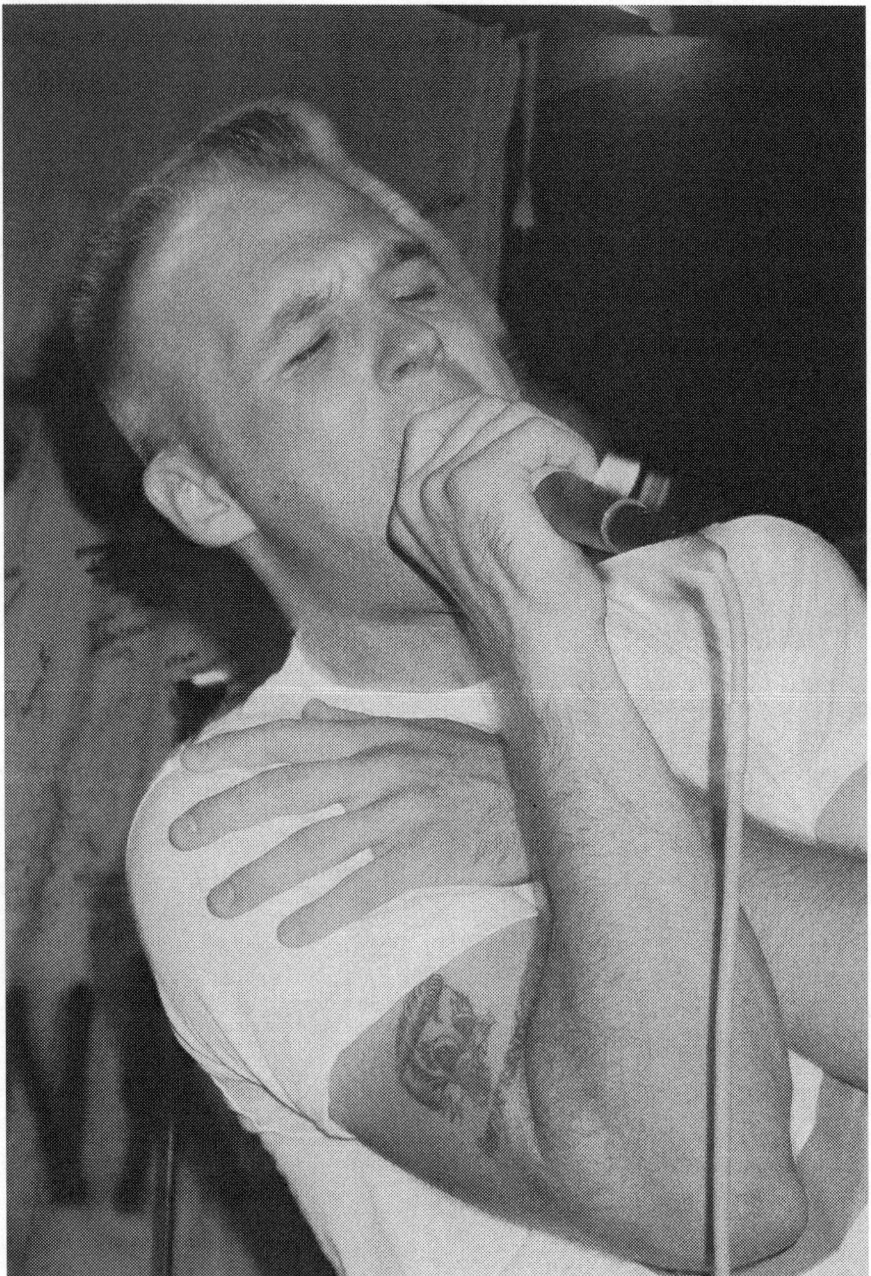

Glenn Goodman at UltraSound
(Photo—Sue Newhouses)

Thursday, August 29, 1991

People are pretty comfortable giving me free advice these days. Family, friends, acquaintances, co-workers, complete strangers, new girlfriends. No one is immune.

Here are the things we really need to do if we "really want to make it":

"You guys are great, but you really need to get a new singer."

"You guys are great, but you really need to get a new bass player."

"You guys are great, but you really need to get a new manager."

"You guys are great, but you really need to make a video."

You guys are great, but you really need to take vocal lessons."

"You guys are great, but you really shouldn't play that song."

"You guys are great, but you really need to write more songs."

"You guys are great, but you really need to have a deejay in the band."

"You guys are great, but you really waste too much time between songs."

"You guys are great, but you should really play this song."

"You guys are great, but you really need to put out a CD."

"You guys are great, but you really need to tour Canada."

At least so far, we really don't need to get a new drummer or a new guitar player.

Thank God.

It really does my head in.

NIAGARA HOUSE, TORONTO—w/ The Coles, Portable Ethnic Taxi

Friday, August 30, 1991

The Niagara House is a long empty room with checker-board floors. Not too far away is the Queen Street Mental Health Center. Although we sold out Toronto's premier club just over a week ago, tonight our audience consists of little more than the Coles and a band from Montreal called Portable Ethnic Taxi.

At UltraSound, the Rheostatics are playing back-to-back shows. I guess that means we're not the flavour of this particular week.

The streets are full of crazies. A prostitute is giving head to a john in Trinity Bellwoods Park. Even though he sliced his leg open on a freezer door near the stage, Rich and the rest of the Coles are jumping around in a boat that's parked on the corner of Richmond and Walnut.

I've got to work in the morning so I'm bailing early. I leave as all three bands go back on stage to jam together. They finish the night with a rendition of *Jane Says.*

I'm not missing anything. We'll do all this again tomorrow night at the Marquee.

This time with Voodoo Chicken.

THE MARQUEE, TORONTO—w/ Voodoo Chicken, Scam Artists

Saturday, August 31, 1991

"Can I have your phone number?" asks the cute bartender.

Steve pulls his left hand out from under his right arm to reveal his wedding ring. He smiles and walks away.

In the background, Glenn and Adam howl with laughter. They'd put the cute bartender up to it. She didn't want to do it but they bugged her until she agreed.

You see, at our shows, Steve has a habit of hiding his wedding-ring-hand beneath his right arm.

Glenn and Adam wanted to see what he'd do if a hot bartender asked for his phone number while Damyana wasn't around. Not surprisingly, Steve passed the test.

Tonight's attendance is still sparse, but not as bad as last night's. In hindsight, we probably should have waited a month or so before booking another show, but we're too afraid of turning down opportunities. There's a lot of competition out there.

With us tonight are Brampton's Scam Artists, and a band called Voodoo Chicken who are made up of ex-M.I.U. members.

We have no idea what to expect from Voodoo Chicken when they wheel a covered catering cart onto the stage. We're amazed to see their singer burst out of it during their first song. After that, it's impossible to look away for fear of missing what they'll do next.

After playing Public Enemy's *Channel Zero*, they end their set by raffling a dream date with their drummer Shawn Connury (no relation). Damyana wins, but like Steve earlier, she resists the temptation.

Voodoo Chicken is going to be hard to follow.

CFNY SPOTLIGHT—THE STREETS OF ONTARIO

Sunday, September 1, 1991

Hal Harbour:

"CFNY 102.1 . . . the Streets of Ontario . . .

Music by the Corndogs, taken from their latest release called What the Hell is Going On? . . . No Boss . . .

Before that, Thomas Trio and the Red Albino, creating quite a critical stir for themselves in the Toronto area since they've been here performing live around town. They are one band to check out live.

Speaking of live, the Discovery Music Mobile was out there, recording live music on the Toronto scene and on August 22nd, we had a night of Bramchester music featuring the Coles, the Smalltown Preachers and the "Best Looking Band on the Face of the Planet", the Marvelous Beauhunks.

We'll have music from that show next . . ."

POST-MORTEM—THE WHITE ROOM, WHITBY

Sunday, September 1, 1991

We finally have a copy of the UltraSound show from CFNY. Scotty's transferring it from DAT to cassette so we can each have a copy of our triumphant night for posterity. At the very least it should be good for impressing girls.

We listen to Hal Harbour's impassioned introduction of the band. Then we wait for Steve to start *TYNL*. Then we wait some more. He's fiddling with his guitar and Glenn and I are talking over each other, trying to fill the awkward silence. A full minute passes before Steve is ready to start the song. It seems like an eternity. This isn't how I remember it at all.

I wince, painfully.

We go straight from *TYNL* into *My Mind Goes Round In Circles*. There's a few high notes that Glenn struggles with, but for the most part we sound good.

Crisis averted.

Except now there's another full minute of Glenn and me cracking wise while Steve's back to tuning his guitar again. Sixty-five seconds of silence on stage, in a room full of drunken punters, is like an hour anywhere else.

I catch myself wincing again.

Happy Together by the Jam comes and goes. Only twenty seconds between songs this time. That's not so bad. Glenn introduces *Kickin'*

Around as a song that we've just finished recording in the studio. He doesn't sound likes he's all too bright. I'm chirping something in the background and I sound like Glenn's less intelligent brother.

Now, I feel embarrassed.

This pattern goes on and on. Each song ending is followed by Steve compulsively tuning up while Glenn and I fill the silence with witty banter. In the cold light of day, we sound positively moronic. At one point, Steve takes more than two full minutes to get his gear back up to spec for the next song. It's torturous.

I want to crawl under the rug and stay there until the pain goes away. The only one who doesn't come off sounding like a complete prat over the course of fifteen songs is Adam, and that's only because we've taken his mike away.

Both Scotty and his mate Dave Parry (our new vocal teacher) tell us that we sound good musically, but we've got a lot of work to do on our presentation. Dave in particular warns us about swearing on stage after he hears Glenn say, "It's hot as a fuck up here," on tape.

"If I was an A&R guy from a record company and I heard that, I'd pour my drink on the floor and walk out," he says.

With that, I know that we've blown it, but good.

This is all happening way too fast for me.

ULTRASOUND SET LIST

Thursday, August 22, 1991

* = time between songs

Hal Harbour Introduction

* 00:54

TYNL—Marvelous Beauhunks

* 00:00

My Mind Goes Round in Circles—Squire

* 1:05

Happy Together—the Jam

* 00:20

Kickin' Around—Marvelous Beauhunks

* 1:12

A Wish Away—Wonderstuff

* 00:34

City Asleep—Marvelous Beauhunks

* 2:11

We Gotta Get Out of This Place—the Animals

* 00:59

Think It Over—Marvelous Beauhunks

* 00:54

Pictures and Tears—Marvelous Beauhunks

* 1:37

Fantasy Merry-Go-Round—Marvelous Beauhunks

* 00:15

Nice Legs (Shame About Her Face)—the Monks

* 00:58

Little Bitch—the Specials

* 00:50

Debbie Jones—Squire

ENCORES

Give Me More—Wonderstuff

* 00:16

Pressure Drop—the Clash

YOU BETTER TELL THAT GIRL TO SHUT UP

Wednesday, September 4, 1991

England's Transvision Vamp is touring their new album, *Little Magnets Versus The Bubble Of Babble*. A few years ago, they were a big deal when their record, *Velveteen* was number one in the UK charts. I don't know anything about them other than their song, *Tell That Girl to Shut Up*.

I do know this though. They're at Lee's Palace tonight and the Marvelous Beauhunks are playing support. A new set of doors has swung wide open, and allowed us to pass through without paying the toll. The street buzz on us has reached a state of fever pitch. So say the promoters at MCA Concerts and CFNY who booked us for the gig. Me, I'm not so sure. But regardless, I'm glad to be here.

As we pull in behind Lee's and start to unload, Derek nods toward the fire escape. Sitting there like a punk Marilyn Monroe is Wendy James, bottle-blonde singer for Transvision Vamp. Beside her, wearing no shirt and what Adam refers to as a "Sid Vicious heroin bandage" on his arm, is their emaciated guitarist, Nick Sayer. Supposedly an item, and seemingly lost in their own world, they pay us no mind as we hump our gear through the doors.

Inside, Lee's is humming. Onstage, TV's bass and drum tech are jamming as the engineer works the sound board. Another roadie mikes a Fender stack and makes adjustments. We watch with genuine interest. So this is how a bona fide English road crew makes things cozy for an international, chart-topping band.

We drop our equipment on the floor in front of the stage. We chat with the road manager and the guitar technician. I begin the arduous process of reassembling my drum kit so it's ready for when they tell us to move it onstage. The drum tech makes his way down from checking Transvision Vamp's drum noises and joins in the conversation. They're all nice guys and happy to field our questions about Paul Weller. The road manager's worked with Billy Idol in the past but that doesn't cut any ice with us.

Sitting down behind my half-built kit, the drum tech starts to absently beat a quiet tattoo on my toms. He's an unassuming geezer and has been nothing but friendly and polite. I try to be funny and bark at him.

"Oi! Off the kit!"

I startle him and he quickly jumps off. He apologizes profusely as I try to explain that I was only joking with him.

I feel like a colossal dick.

Transvision Vamp comes out to do their sound check. The drum tech is back on stage playing with them. He's their fucking drummer. What's bigger than colossal? Gargantuan?

Derek arranges for us to have a formal introduction with Wendy James. She's only my age but, up close and without all the make-up, I'm shocked at how shovel-beaten she looks. Civil but distant, Wendy says she's happy to make our acquaintance. Within a minute, she fades off into a booth and begins putting pen to paper. She could be composing lyrics, but the forlorn look on her face lends itself to the idea that she's writing letters home. Adam admits to being unsettled by the image of loneliness she projects.

At show time, Lee's is packed. Up until now, the biggest crowd we've been in front of has been 350. I'm guessing that there's a thousand punters here tonight. To see Transvision Vamp.

And us.

I can barely make it to the bar.

From our first song, *TYNL* again, things don't feel right. We don't have the usual MBH attitude and swagger. Tonight, we're just four kids from Oshawa who are out of their depth. Steve looks like he's lost all confidence and without him leading the charge, the rest of us can't find our balance. When he announces to the punters not to worry, that Transvision Vamp will be on soon, it's an admission of defeat.

We go into *Nice Legs* and things come to a head. Adam ventures off the stage and out onto the big house speakers. Some bright spark thinks it's hilarious to shake the speakers, hoping to make Adam fall off.

While Adam shuffles back to the safety of the stage, I go into my usual drum acrobatics. During the breakdown, I stand on top of my drum seat and play out the rest of the song. This move is a guaranteed crowd-pleaser. Tonight is no exception.

When *Nice Legs* ends, I plant my feet back on terra firma. Victory is mine.

I take a step backwards and right into the Fender stack belonging to Transvision Vamp's Nick Sayer. It falls back against the wall at a forty-five degree angle.

Like a banshee, their guitar tech is stage left, hissing at me with murder in his voice.

"WANKER! GET OFF THE STAGE—YOU FUCKING CUNT!"

What's the difference between mortification and humiliation?

Not a goddamn thing.

Glenn looks back at me, shrugs, and says, "Fuck it. Keep playing."

After two more songs, including the now-ubiquitous *Fantasy Merry-Go-Round*, we slink off stage, tails firmly between legs.

We grab some beers, sulk and wonder out loud for the first time that we might actually be in over our heads. Then we play the blame game. You did this. You didn't do that. You're ruining it for all of us. You're a cunt. Well you're a bigger cunt.

Transvision Vamp's guitar tech comes over to where I'm standing. He apologizes for overreacting. That was nice of him, but the wind is already out of my sails.

I just want to go home.

Adam Graham at Lee's Palace
(Photo—Sue Newhouses)

THE APOCALYPSE—w/ SKAFACE, Cadillac Bill & the Creeping Bent

Friday, September 13, 1991

Black cats, broken mirrors, walking under ladders.

Nothing beats Friday the 13th for bad luck.

Steve and I are standing in Glenn's bedroom, looking at him as he lies beneath his blankets.

"I can't play tonight. I'm sick," he moans.

We're due at the Apocalypse Club in little more than an hour-and-a-half. NOW Magazine has us listed as part of a "Skanking Ska-Mod-Garage Triple Bill." There's a car and a truck full of equipment ready to make the trip to Little Italy's seedy underbelly. This is the first we're hearing of Glenn's illness.

Steve and I look at each other. We've got no choice but to attempt the gig without Glenn. When he hears that the show will go on without him, Glenn suddenly decides that he'll come along just in case he feels well enough to sing. Minutes later we're rolling down the 401 with Glenn bundled in the back seat, fast asleep.

The Apocalypse is low-ceilinged and poorly lit. There's a dangerous vibe floating in the air, exacerbated by the ravings of a transient-looking fellow who's brandishing a flick-knife. As he walks through the crowd, his cursing and knife-wielding antics cut him a wide swath. True to the surplus of kitted out Vespas and Lambretta's lined up out front, tonight's audience is made up of a large contingent of skinheads and scooter boys.

With Glenn asleep in the parking lot, Steve and I scramble to trade-off who's going to sing lead on what songs. We practice vocal scales while Adam digs into his band-bag for paper, markers, and gaffer tape. Say what you will about Adam, but the guy's always prepared. Tylenol, nail clippers, pliers, plectrums, guitar strings . . . you name it, he carries a supply of it in an old army sack. By the time Steve and I are sufficiently warmed up, he's got three set-lists ready to go.

Up first are Cadillac Bill and the Creeping Bent, representing the "Garage" part of the bill. Their Cramps-tinged rockabilly goes largely under-appreciated by the braces and boots crowd. When they finish, we have a few minutes to switch over the backline and get ready for our Glenn-less set. We're as ready as we're ever going to be, given that we're firing on three cylinders.

Suddenly, there's a smoky figure at the top of the stairs. Backlit by streetlamps, Glenn "Gooders" Goodman steps out of the fog. In my mind, the theme from the Good, the Bad and the Ugly is playing. Glenn saunters down the black staircase, looking every inch the confident rock and roll star with his Man U scarf tied casually around his neck. He's sound as a pound and glad-handing the punters. He doesn't have a care in the world.

We're back in business.

Buoyed by our relief at Glenn's unexpected appearance, we're shiny and new again. We play with a spirit and energy that's been unseen seen since the El Mocambo show, when we were just happy to be in a band. Steve leaps into the crowd for a guitar solo and he's swallowed up. Eventually he re-emerges, looking a little stunned. He hadn't expected that. Grinning at me, he climbs back on stage and we continue to give one of our best performances. Our set finishes with Gorilla Phil bodlly ejecting invaders from the stage. What started out as a disaster has turned into one of our stand-out nights as a band.

It's our turn to relax and have a few pints as SKAFACE closes the night. They put on a great show as usual, and the skinheads go mad for it.

Friday the 13th.

Who knew?

Tuesday, September 17, 1991

At rehearsal tonight, Glenn let it slip that he hadn't actually been sick on Friday. He'd been up all night drinking brandy with Davy.

"I don't know what you guys are so pissed off about," he said.

Wednesday, September 18, 1991

It was Steve's turn to make the posters, so here we are in Peterborough with some tape and a staple-gun. Saturday is officially the Marvelous Beauhunks "Hide Your Daughters Tour" at the Underdog.

It's a great night to hit the streets. Cool and brisk with that brand-new-school-year vibe in the air. More and more, I've been getting the itch to go to university. There's got to be life past the Marvelous Beauhunks. I'm not sure what it is, but I think I might like to be a teacher.

Steve and I stop for a pint and then head south down the one-fifteen. I can see the lights of Oshawa off in the distance.

I feel restless.

MARVELOUS BEAUHUNKS

The Peterborough Examiner, Wednesday, September 18, 1991

Tracy Hanes

On Saturday night, Oshawa's ***Marvelous Beauhunks*** *make a return visit to the Underdog, which drummer Steve Wright and bassist Adam Graham claim is "the place we like playing most. It's a big party."*

The group, which facetiously calls itself "the best looking band in the world", hails from South Oshawa—"the tough end of town . . . the other side of the tracks," according to Wright and Graham.

And as Oshawa has not exactly been a rich breeding ground for talent, ("it's us and the Killer Dwarfs," says Graham), the Beauhunks have earned the reputation of "small town boys make good."

The Beauhunks sound is distinctively '60s British flavoured, due to their use of vintage Rickenbacker guitar, although their influences are diverse, ranging from the Beatles to more contemporary bands like the Clash and the Jam.

Their single, Fantasy Merry-Go-Round is included on the 1991 CFNY Modern Music compact disc and peaked at number 16 on CFNY charts, which "is impressive for us." Their song has also been played on college radio, CBC and an alternative B.C. station.

The band has been getting steady work in Toronto clubs and is set to release a six song EP this fall. Fans may also be interested in the band's "new line of casual-wear": t-shirts which sell for $12 at the gigs.

Admission is $3 to Saturday's show. Opening will be Voodoo Chicken, which Wright and Graham claim are "total entertainers. They're really comedic, very visual."

TRENT RADIO—HIDE YOUR DAUGHTERS TOUR

Saturday, September 21, 1991

I'm working today but that doesn't stop the other guys from going early to Peterborough.

As part of the promotion for tonight's gig, Derek's arranged an on-air interview at Trent Radio.

There's no time limit for them to be there, so they play records, take phone calls, and eventually run out of things to talk about.

The conversation eventually degenerates into a debate about the respective size of their Doctor Martens.

Sadly, the deejay seems almost disappointed when they leave.

THE UNDERDOG, PETERBOROUGH (HIDE YOUR DAUGHTERS TOUR) w/ Voodoo Chicken

Saturday, September 21, 1991

The Underdog is unanimously our favourite venue. We get the best crowds and the place is always packed. When you take the Red Dog Buffet into account, it's also the most lucrative.

I've driven to Peterborough alone and arranged for Maria to meet me here before the show. She's brought one of her university girlfriends who's pals with the drummer from I Mother Earth. They've been in a record company feeding frenzy and are about to be signed. Hearing about it eats me up with jealousy. The Marvelous Beauhunks have been all over the radio and half-way up the Top 30 without even a nibble from the lowest-level record company.

Voodoo Chicken are back with us and, although they're not quite as funny as they were at the Marquee, they're still pretty hilarious. When they finish their set, it's our turn. Derek plays deejay while the crowd settles in. We hear our cue, the soulful *Green Onions* by Booker T. and the MGs, and we take the stage.

Our set is solid but uneventful. I'm happy for the lack of drama for a change. There's a Goth girl from Montreal that's been hanging around the musicians, looking for any taker. She doesn't find one. She's last seen wandering the streets of Peterborough in search of god-knows-what.

Maria's suspicious of my motivations for wanting to spend the night without her. She keeps insisting that it's not that far to drive home. She's missing the point. I want to stay so I can get legless with my mates.

"I'm a musician," I think to myself. "This is what I do."

Deal with it.

Glenn Goodman at the Underdog
(Photo—Adam Graham Collection)

Stephen Closs, Stephen Wright at the Underdog
(Photo—Adam Graham Collection)

THE MBH TATTOO

Sunday, September 22, 1991

The voice your hearing now belongs to esteemed Marvelous Beauhunks manager, Derek Supryka.

Take it away Derek.

This is time for a little detour. Now that we're travelling a bit, the arrangements always change regarding who goes where, with whom and when. Tensions have surfaced about unaccompanied boys on the road, and the ladies are exercising a lot more spirit in their demands for their beloveds. On this trip to Peterborough, Glenn's flying solo, and he and I are riding together in his old VW. This works out well since we've devised a little side trip.

A co-worker at the supermarket knows someone who has a tattoo kit at his house. He lives out in the sticks near where we are for the gig. So, in the tradition of our prior trips to Peterborough, we ripped it up last night. This morning we woke up and all went our separate ways, unified in our 'I think I'm still drunk' haze.

Now Glenn and I have set out for our collective tattoo adventure. We arrange to meet our co-worker and then go to the tattoo guy's house. Driving there, we're excited about getting tattooed and having it not cost a fortune. We're really keen since both of us have made our own designs, and given them to our co-worker to give to the guy in advance, so he can study them.

Glenn has decided to take what can only be considered one of the greatest leaps of faith known to mankind—to get the name of his band tattooed on his arm. He's devised a really simple, yet elegant 'MBH' and he wants it nested between the two tattoos he's already got.

Goodman's been getting inked for a few years now and he's got fucking nice works on him already. This is sensible as it ties the two tattoos together nicely. Me, on the other hand, I want a small blue swallow—a sign of peace and hope. I had done a design and got it perfect. All he needs to do is to make a transfer of it, stick it on my arm and follow the lines. Easy as piss.

We roll up on the dude's house and "Ping!" there's warning sound number one in my head for the coming apocalypse—it's a total fucking dump on the outside.

"Ping! Ping!" Oh-oh, there goes number two. It's a dump on the inside as well.

Mud and dirt are everywhere . . .

The dishes are piled to the moon . . .

Motorcycle parts have drifted from the yard to inside the house . . .

The dude is basically in his pyjamas still . . .

But he smells drunk . . .

Fuck, his whole house smells drunk . . .

Oh shit, he actually has a drink on the go . . .

Oh my fuck, he has two drinks on the go and one looks like it's from last night . . .

Did he just tear the filter off his smoke and spit it onto his own kitchen floor??

When he offers us tea, he tries to rinse a glass out but gives up before trying soap . . .

Just as I am thinking to myself; "Why am I here . . . ?" the dude asks, "Why are you here . . . ?"

He can't find either of the designs we've given him in advance . . .

His attempted MBH sketch looked like I put a pencil in my ass cheeks and did it . . .

My inner Rembrandt takes a stab at doing an MBH sketch on the spot . . .

My sketch pleases Glenn but the dude can't find the stencil supplies to get it onto his arm . . .

The dude says he'll freestyle. To my surprise, Goodman agrees. Fuck. Glenn's still drunk from yesterday and he's been driving for over an hour . . .

To shave Glenn's arm, he uses a pink Lady Shave disposable that has been previously enjoyed . . .

His wife comes out and that hammers home the point about the razor. Glenn is now sober. Disturbingly sober . . .

The guy doesn't change the needle on the tattoo gun . . .

When I mention it to him, he cleans it with spit. I guess he's really fucking wasted if he thinks his spit has so much alcohol in it, that it can sterilize a tattoo gun . . .

I ask him about AIDS and he thinks I mean little chocolates for fat people . . .

At this point, I officially put off my tattoo indefinitely. I am so glad he can't find my design since it gives me all the excuse I need to bail out of it. Poor Glenn isn't so lucky and I bet he wishes he was anywhere but here right now . . .

Bzzzzzzzzzzz . . . Bzzzzz . . . Bbbbzzzzzz. And it's done . . .

Glenn can't see it as it's upside down for him. He immediately turns to me and looks for a sign of approval. It never comes. My nervous system has just totally shut down. It seems like forever and he finally says, "Well, how does it look?"

It looks like someone has pissed an MBH in the snow. Not someone who's spent all his spare time practicing writing MBH in the snow to get good at it, but someone who's gotten so wasted that he pissed MBH on someone's yard and it turned out to be his own. Yes. Like someone has pissed an unceremonious MBH into the snow and then fused it onto Glenn's arm.

By now, Glenn is wise and he's in the can, which is also a fucking dirty mess . . . and he's mad. Really, really fucking pissed. But he's smart enough to realize that the biker guy that just did his tattoo doesn't have the sense of appreciation for clean straight lines and well rounded curves that we do. So he keeps it buttoned. We strategize in the toilet how we can cut a path for escape and, within five minutes, we're beating a hasty retreat

When all is said and done, the moral of the story is this:

Like the tattoo of your lover's name, the band related tattoo has a very high statistical rate of failure attached to it. Not only do you run the risk of having the ink of an ex's name on you forever, you run the risk of encountering a plethora of health and safety issues.

Choosing to make this decision, to permanently alter your appearance in this way, is a bold gambit that does not always pay any dividends.

In this case, for anyone other than Glenn, the only dividends are cheap laughs.

STRATENGERS, TORONTO—w/ Pasty White Boys

Thursday, September 26, 1991

Aw, c'mon. Stratengers again?

I thought we were done with this place. Can't Derek do any better? And why are we playing a Thursday night instead of a Friday or Saturday?

I'm in a foul mood. Our friend Kerri is singing in the band that's playing support tonight, Pasty White Boys. I was only half kidding when I told her that a chick singer would open for us over my dead body. But I do have to admit that she looks good in her evening gloves, black dress and combat boots.

Despite trying hard, the band is nothing special. The drummer's playing is holding them back. He's enthusiastic but inexperienced. If they had a stronger engine, the Pasty White Boys might stand a better chance.

While they play, I make my way to the upper level. Sitting at a table are a bunch of Kerri's girlfriends from Oshawa. I stop by to say hi. No one acknowledges me as I stand there in front of them for what feels like an eternity. They fucking blank me.

Under a black cloud, I wander back downstairs. Adam and I go outside and sit on the steps next to the club. The Pasty White Boys finish up their last song.

Before too long, the bass player and guitarist from the Pasty's come through the door, and pass by us on the street.

"What did you just say to me?" I ask the Pasty bass player.

"What?" he replies.

"What did you just fucking say to me?" I ask again, more aggressively this time.

"I didn't say anything to you," he says.

"I fucking heard you call me something," I insist, puffing myself up for maximum intimidation.

"I didn't call you anything, man. Jesus Christ! Calm down," says Pasty Bass as he walks away.

"You better not have," I warn, feeling like an idiot.

Adam and I head back inside and play our set.

T&A (TEACHING AND ASSISTING)

October 1991

More and more, I'm convinced that it's my calling to become a teacher.

My aunt's arranged for me to do some volunteer teacher-assisting at my cousin's elementary school.

A few days into it, my dreams of shaping young minds are shattered. While I work yard-duty, I'm powerless as second-graders pummel me with rocks and stones.

"You can't touch us," they taunt me. "Or, you'll go to jail."

"I may do time," I think to myself, "but you won't be around to see it."

The school bell rings, the kids line up and I rethink my future.

Back to square one.

COFFEE-MAKER

October 1991

We need some new original material but we've hit a creative block. In a group effort during rehearsal, we've written a song called Coffee-Maker.

Steve came up with a tune and we all took turns throwing out random lyrics while Glenn wrote them down.

Here they are:

Verse 1:
She is my coffee-maker
She is my undertaker
She is my love-maker
She's my coffee-maker
She's my coffee-maker

Verse 2:
My coffee-maker sets me free
She takes me where I wanna be
She's my coffee-maker
She's my coffee-maker

Chorus:
A place where my love drink flows
She is my coffee-maker

Verse 3:
Once, twice, three times Melita
After this I'll never see her

When she says "Hey Bob"
I say "Nabob"
She's my coffee-maker
She's my coffee-maker

This is what passes for a Marvelous Beauhunks song these days.

SEXIST BAND RECEIVES RADIO PUBLICITY

The Arthur, Volume 26, Issue 4 (Trent University Campus Paper)
October 1, 1991

Editors:

On Thursday, Sept. 19, I was on my way to the Three Seconds to Think show at the PR Dining Hall. At the time, I was setting up for the gig thinking about the celebrators of the Take Back the Night march that might come to the dining hall. Outside the Hangman was a poster advertising the up and coming Marvelous Beauhunks Red Dog gig. I was confused, then outraged in light of that particular day, to see one quote on the poster that said: "The Hide your Daughters Tour".

You've got to ask yourself, "Why?" I have a big problem with the implications of such a motto. I cannot justify such a statement in any positive sense. The result is sexist and an abuse of public space.

Dealing with such a statement is problematic. Freedom of speech and thought enable us as people to protect ourselves from the implements of power and control. At the same time, does the freedom of speech permit us to be abusive and sexist in the public domain?

On Friday, Sept. 27, it came to my attention that this same band was being provided the production of a cart at Tent Radio for this same up and coming gig. I later heard that this band was given an on air interview to publicize the gig. Is anyone catching on?

Last school year, Trent Radio saw the realities of such sexism and acted accordingly to "correct" the situation. The events were emotional and Trent Radio has to be commended for acting on a political principle.

The station seems now to be in a period of healing and regrouping from a previous situation.

I would like to ask Trent Radio if they feel that such a promotion is worth the fee that the Red Dog provides to support such events?

Secondly, I see such an instance as a precedent for the new board and operation. Does such an endorsement mean that we can look forward to more events of this calibre?

Thirdly, I would like for Trent Radio to publicize the particulars of this event's promotion agreement with Red Dog Ray so that all bands playing at the Red Dog will be aware of what they must do to ensure adequate radio support.

Thank you for reading this.

[redacted]

Peterborough resident

IN SISTERHOOD

The Arthur, Volume 26, Issue 5 (Trent University Campus Paper) October 8, 1991

Editors:

I am writing to commend [redacted] on his vigilance and commitment to making Trent Radio a "sexist-free zone."

This year, Trent Radio is making every effort to provide non-sexist, non-racist, non-homophobic programming.

Needless to say, it is a huge undertaking and sometimes we may not catch everything. However, people like yourself, [redacted] make it easier to fulfill our commitment to this type of programming. Your letter reaffirms our belief that sexism has no place on the airwaves—or anywhere else.

In regard to ensuring adequate support for local talent, Trent Radio is willing to provide studio space for cart production. Whether you choose to do promotion through Red Dog Ray or to deal directly with Trent Radio, the space remains yours for the taking.

Sincerely,

[redacted]

Program Director, Trent Radio

P.S. A big thanx to everyone who is contributing their ideas, time and energy to Trent Radio this year.

RE: SEXIST BAND RECEIVES RADIO PUBLICITY

The Arthur, Volume 26, Issue 6 (Trent University Campus Paper) October 15, 1991

Editors:

I agree with [redacted] *that the poster outside the Hangman, and all over Peterborough advertising the Marvelous Beauhunks on their "Hide Your Daughters Tour" was/is extremely sexist, and I too found it to be offensive.*

A week later, the offensive poster was for the Healthy Libido's gig at the Underdog. I walked down the street, upon discovering these posters, marker in hand, de-facing or rather re-facing the poster with "This poster objectifies women" and "Sexist Shit."

Annually, Spring Break posters have been put up that have also been identified as degrading women.

During "Homecoming" week, or whatever it is, there was a portable signboard lit up, advertising the "Old Boys Rugby Game", referring to the Trent alumni. Are there any such events remotely similar that celebrate the "Old Girls" from Trent or are there any women alumni?

The point I'm trying to make here is that there are examples in our culture and even Peterborough's smug "alternative" or "counterculture" of material that reflects sexist attitudes. It is important to identify this material and show the institutions that produce them that we will not accept this attitude, be it the Marvelous Beauhunks or Mediacom.

However, I think [redacted] *is making a big mistake and blaming the new board at Trent Radio for advertising the Marvelous Beauhunks. The Board of Directors cannot act as a police force, censoring everything that goes on the air. What they can and have done (as I understand it) is create a false promise of performance that supports affirmative action. Things like making the station more accessible to those groups whose voices are not heard in mainstream media, one example being women. Another responsibility of the board is to hold people accountable for what they say on the airwaves. It is important that people who find what they hear on the radio to be racist, sexist, homophobic etc. get in touch with the board. I'm sure they would be more than happy to investigate the situation and rectify it. (By the way, I am speaking out not as a representative of Trent Radio but as a former programmer and former member of Women's Voice).*

I question what motivated [redacted] to write an article to Arthur that, as I see it, condemns Trent Radio and the Board of Directors as a whole. He says that he "see(s) such an instance (providing advertising for a band that produces sexist offensive posters) as a precedent for the new board and operation." Ask [redacted] if he blamed the Board of Directors for the operation for the "Naked Ladies in the Basement" scandal (see past issues of Arthur for details)? Did he pass judgment on anyone at this time last year? It seems to me that his letter to the editor is another example of where men do a job and screw-up and other men in the "Boys Club" label them as incompetent in some way.

I wonder if [redacted] has another bone to pick with Trent Radio aside from all this stuff about sexism. Whether or not he does, he's still using a different set of values to judge this board as he would have to judge last year's board-members and former members of Trent Radio.

I'd like to ask [redacted] if he was "shocked" because he, with little or no knowledge of the history or involvement with Trent Radio, judges Trent Radio or was he, with a great deal of history and involvement with Trent Radio judging Trent radio with a different set of values as he would have over last year's board? Was this letter to the editor an attack on current radio using sexism as a vehicle?

[redacted]

P.S. I would encourage anyone who has a complaint with the programming of Trent Radio being sexist, racist, homophobic etc. to contact the board stating the date and time which you heard it.

RADIO INTERVIEW—CIUT

Monday, October 14, 1991

We're doing an on on-air interview/performance at CIUT.

The deejay's condescending and keeps referring to us as the Marvelous "Boo-hunks." We're not happy about it but we keep it buttoned. I keep my eye on Steve just in case.

After we play acoustic versions of *Fantasy Merry-Go-Round* and *Coffee-Maker*, the deejay starts in with the "Boo-hunk" shit again.

Adam asks the deejay if he'll be as funny once we beat the fuck out of him, live on the air.

The interview's over.

TONGUE IN CHEEK HUMOUR

The Arthur, Volume 26, Issue 6 (Trent University Campus Paper) October 15, 1991

Editor:

We, the Marvelous Beauhunks, think it's sad to see the likes of [redacted] (Arthur, Vol. 26 #4) judging us from his/her myopic point of view. Rather than condemning something because it doesn't conform to one's own personal set of ideals, [redacted] may in the future try to consider issues in a more Gestalt-like manner. Given a more liberal perspective, [redacted] would have realized that "Hide your Daughters" was as tongue-in-cheek as the band name Marvelous Beauhunks. Quite often, when a particular interest group views the world, humour gets lost amid ideology and condemnation. The same rights to freedoms that enable [redacted] to attend functions as Three Seconds to Think and the "Take Back the Night March" without reprisal, also allow the Marvelous Beauhunks to express our sense of humour in whatever way we see fit. Our collective sense of humour is not malicious and should be taken with a grain of salt. Before succumbing to accusations of sexism, the band would like to invite [redacted] to any of our upcoming shows (check any current issue of Now). Without any direct contact, we would be just as much in err labelling [redacted] as just another Feminist Sympathizer.

The Marvelous Beauhunks do not deal in issues of man vs. woman, black vs. white etc. We are pro-humanity. Period. [redacted] should also promote human welfare, not just one half of it!

The Marvelous Beauhunks appreciate Trent Radio for protecting our freedom of speech, which it is obliged to do under the laws governing Canada. To be accused of being "abusive and sexist in the public domain" is a travesty!

In closing, the band respects [redacted] opinions. We ask only for the same "courtesy." Thank you Trent Radio, Red Dog Ray, and especially the loyal fans who support us. Next time we're in town, bring your daughters! It'll be a blast.

Stephen Closs
Stephen Wright
Glenn Goodman
Adam Graham

Aka: The Marvelous Beauhunks

P.S. What's wrong with being sexy?

Friday, October 18, 1991

We've been turned down for a FACTOR grant to do a video for *Fantasy Merry-Go-Round.*

Back in September, Steve and I had gone to see a film producer that we found in the back of NOW magazine. He wrote us a treatment with the usual stuff like the band playing live while outstretched hands reach for us. Somewhere in the background, is the girl on the merry-go-round. Predictable stuff but who cares? It met with the requirements. We just wanted a video to capitalize on our momentum while we still had some.

We signed off on the treatment and the producer sent it off to FACTOR. He thought it'd be an easy win given that we're getting plenty of airplay from CFNY.

No dice.

To add insult to injury, the Barenaked Ladies have been given a grant to do a video for Bruce Cockburn's *Lovers in a Dangerous Time.* FACTOR would rather give these clowns money for a cover song instead of financing our original stuff?

Fuck those guys.

Hey Bruce Cockburn—enjoy your bank account.

If I had a rocket-launcher . . .

MARVELOUS BULLHEADS, BOYS OF PRIVILEGE

The Arthur, Volume 26, Issue 7 (Trent University Campus Paper)
October 29, 1991

Editors:

It's very difficult for me to write this letter to the Marvelous Beauhunks. Every sentence of their response to [redacted] offends and injures me as a woman.

The Marvelous Beauhunks think it's "sad" that [redacted] judges them by "his/her own myopic point of view . . ." and feel that [redacted] should adopt a more "liberal perspective" before condemning sexism. They (those oh so Marvelous Beauhunks) are concerned that "when a particular interest group views the world, humour gets lost amid ideology and condemnation".

If your white, male, humour suffers as a result of my safety then so be it. There is nothing funny about "hide your daughters." Why would women choose to hide or why would parents choose to force them into hiding? Implicit in your sexist humour is the real FEAR that women live with constantly. Were you implying that you were going to harm us or that some other man would probably harm us?

Furthermore, you imply in your oh so funny remarks ("Hide your Daughters" or "Bring your Daughter's") that women have no control over their own destiny. This is not funny either. It too, is often a reality for us. Fighting sexism is one way women can take back control of our destiny.

Your collective sense of humour is malicious and you need to know that. I am a woman and I'm very clear about what is malicious to me and what isn't. Listen to me. I know that I speak for many others.

[redacted] did not "succumb to accusations of sexism", he rose above and risked his white male privilege by naming and condemning your lack of sensitivity toward women.

It doesn't surprise me that the Marvelous Beauhunks "do not deal in issues of men versus women black versus white etc."—you don't have to. That is what your white male supremacy looks like. (Just in case you take it for granted). Condemning sexism does not, as you suggest, promote human welfare for only one half of the population. The fact that you would see it that way implies that your welfare depends on the degradation of women.

In closing, I must question the integrity of Trent Radio and Red Dog Ray for having promoted the Marvelous Beauhunks and for not taking a public stand on sexism and violence against women. Your silence and complicity in this matter scares me.

[redacted]

P.S. I will personally tell everyone I know NOT to ever go see THE Marvelous Bullheads.

P.P.S. I noticed you quote Spinal Tap in your postscript. That movie was a brilliant expose of the sexism and idiocy of the mainstream music industry. Get it?

THE ALAN ALDA SENSITIVE GUY TOUR THE UNDERDOG, PETERBOROUGH w/ All Good Children

Friday, November 1, 1991

Tonight's our first trip back to Peterborough since the "Hide Your Daughters Tour." I was expecting a bit of a furor over our penis-party, but there's been barely a mention of it since we got here.

We're playing support for a band from Hamilton called All Good Children. Why we're opening for these guys in a place that we can pack on our own, is a mystery to me. It's just one more instance of management making a cock-up of things.

Derek's been doing some damage control and has invited [redacted] and a plus-one to the show as our guests. Once she meets us in person, she'll see that we're not the monsters she's made us out to be.

When [redacted] and her friend get here, we all shake hands and make peace. By the time I walk away from the conversation, Glenn's already hitting on her.

It's not like we can just smack him on the nose with a rolled-up newspaper or something.

GET YOUR SHIT TOGETHER BEAUHUNKS

The Arthur, Volume 26, Issue 8 (Trent University Campus Paper) November 5, 1991

Editors:

In last week's Arthur, the self-declared Marvelous Beauhunks wrote objecting to [redacted] statement that calling a tour the "Hide your Daughters Tour" was sexist and offensive. Telling Peterborough to hide their daughters is offensive—it suggests they are coming to rape and pillage.

In their letter, they claim to respect [redacted] opinions. The Flavourless Blockheads have proven that this is not the case by writing on their new poster, "The New Alan Alda Tour, courtesy of [redacted] Productions."

Most bands that come to Peterborough do their best to entertain and please the crowd and are rewarded by lots of dancing and cries for encores. Do we really want to give our money to a band that is insulting both women and individual members of our community? (That's a rhetorical question.)

The Marvelous Blowchunks are also mistaken when they say that Trent Radio is obligated to protect their right to free speech. Trent Radio is not allowed to violate their right to free speech, but they are allowed to make programming decisions. The members of the board, when running for election, made a promise to stop sexism on the air. This is not censorship, this is ethical programming. Reducing sexism, a widespread societal problem, is a formidable task and Trent Radio should be excused for the mistake of airing a cartridge and an interview with the Humourless HoHumms.

I take issue with [redacted] however, claiming that [redacted] is judging the "new board" with a different set of values than he would've the "old board." The new membership of the Trent Radio board this year has made a different set of commitments. Maybe [redacted] should have made it clear he had personal connections with members of the "old boys" on the "old board" but he quite correctly points out this new board's mistakes.

Keep up the good job [redacted], Trent Radio and [redacted]. Get your shit together Beauhunks.

Looking forward to being insulted on their next poster,

[redacted]

P.S. Don't accuse [redacted] of being into censorship—he was at City Hall last Monday in support of postering.

OSHAWA'S OWN MARVELOUS BEAUHUNKS SAY "IT'S ABOUT TIME"

Home Free—Oshawa's Beauhunks are on the road home once again.

Oshawa This Week, Wednesday, November 6, 1991

Oshawa's own Marvelous Beauhunks are finally coming home.

The Oshawa band is playing, for the first time, in front of a home-town crowd on Saturday, at the Star Club. The Beauhunks will open the show for the Cynics.

The group has played a number of shows in Toronto, including a show with international recording artists Transvision Vamp, and in Peterborough, but have yet to play in the Motor City.

. . .

We didn't really say that, did we?

It was probably Glenn.

OSHAWA'S OWN MARVELOUS BEAUHUNKS SAY "IT'S ABOUT TIME"

The Star Club is legendary.

This is where I cut my teeth watching bands like Durango 95, Purple Toads, UIC, the Gruesomes, and the Chesterfield Kings. The drummer for Shadowy Men on a Shadowy Planet tried to sell me his spare kit out in the parking lot when I was 16. Without these groups, I'd have never tried to be in a band myself.

Despite all this, I don't want to play the Star Club. I don't want to play in Oshawa period. I'm outvoted.

To me, the hometown gig isn't an opportunity to show off our success. The hometown gig is an opportunity for people who knew you when you were nothing, to remind you that you're still nothing. They'll make damn sure you don't forget your place in the hierarchy.

The true benchmark of band coolness is directly proportionate to how far the band has had to travel to get to the gig. I'm surprised that I'm the only one that realizes this.

No gets out of Oshawa alive.

THE STAR CLUB, OSHAWA—w/ the Cynics

Saturday, November 9, 1991

The Cynics, from Pittsburgh PA, finish their sound check and whinge that their amps aren't miked. The soundman argues that they're plenty loud, and the room's not that big. They insist until they get their own way.

Compared to other the acts I've seen here, I'm not impressed.

Their drummer is a miserable looking git in black Steelers track pants. He's taking his drums down and moving them off the stage. This causes me some concern. We were told not to bring our drums because we'd be using the Cynics' kit. I continue to watch him, not understanding what's happening.

By the time he gets to the floor tom I ask him, "Hey, can I use your floor tom?"

"No," he replies, dismissively.

"Are you being serious?" I ask, confused.

"Yeah, I'm serious." He says with an attitude.

"But I was told we'd be using your drums tonight." I make sure to keep my tone neutral.

"Well, you're not." He says and walks away.

"So that's how it is." I muse. "Cynics eh? We'll see."

We miss our opportunity to sound-check. Adam and I rocket back to seven-eighty-two to rescue my drums from the basement. Steve and Glenn stay behind to do an interview with Global Television.

My kit goes into the back of the truck fully assembled. Within a half-hour, we have them up on the stage. There's just enough time for a line-check before the club starts to fill. As the home-team, most of the punters are here to see us, not the cynical Cynics.

We start our set and my predictions come true. There's a contingent of Glenn's football friends whose sole purpose here is to make sure we don't forget our place in the social order. Between songs, we're shouted at by long-time Canadians with absurdly thick Scottish brogues.

"Heyyy, Gooodman! Play yerrrr hit! Big rock starrrr! Fookin' wankerrr!"

This goes on between each song until Steve finally has enough and dedicates *Little Bitch* to the ringleader.

"This one's for your fucking sister . . ."

We're ready to give the stage over to the Cynics, but there's one more order of business to attend to.

"You can either stay here and watch the Cynics or you can come with us. We're going to the Ozone," Glenn announces.

A big yell resonates through the Star Club and the crowd files out. Maybe 20 people stay behind to watch the pride of Pittsburgh.

"You should've let us use your drums." I think to myself.

And that, my friends, is one to grow on.

QUESTIONING WHITE MALE PRIVILEGE

The Arthur, Volume 26, Issue 9 (Trent University Campus Paper) November 12, 1991

Re: a ridiculous number of complaints

The Marvelous Beauhunks controversy, over their "sexist" poster, has gone too far. To begin with, look at the name of the band, Marvelous Beauhunks. Are you going to take this literally that these guys think they're a bunch of beer swilling, fun-loving guys out for a good time. Their music and show is based on humour, as was their "Hide your Daughters" poster. I suggest that anyone who does not believe me check out their show and do not judge the band on what [redacted], [redacted] and [redacted] ignorantly believe. I would also like to question my "white male privilege" that [redacted] says that I've been blessed with. Is this the same "white male privilege" that disallows me to walk on the same side of the street at night as a woman, disallows me from disagreeing with minorities for fear being labeled as a racist/sexist pig, and the same privilege that disqualifies me from many jobs, even if I am better qualified, because "minority" quotas must be met. Nice privilege eh? You have to admit that Alan Alda is an outstanding citizen.

[redacted]

P.S. Do not take everything so literally and enjoy life, don't fear it.

SNEAKY DEE'S, TORONTO—w/ Snowdogs, the Coles, Sarcastic Mannequins

Friday, November 15, 1991

Emergency meeting behind Sneaky Dee's.

Glenn's a liability. He's got to go.

Tonight's performance was an embarrassment. He's got no respect for the punters or for Steve, Adam, or I. We're supposed to be a team, but Glenn doesn't care about the team. Glenn cares about Glenn.

From the moment we went on, he was sloppy. The Coles kept waiting for him to topple off the stage. Their drummer said it looked like the only thing keeping Glenn upright were his Doctor Martens.

Tonight, our solution for Glenn's out-of-control behaviour was to have Derek babysit him and keep him away from the booze until our set was over. Derek's interpretation of minding Glenn was to skin-up a spliff while on the way to the Beer Store.

More and more people have been pointing Glenn out as the weak link in the band. It's a sore point for us that he's been missing his vocal lessons. Steve and I still go to ours, as much to set an example for Glenn, as to learn vocal technique. My sessions with Dave Parry consist of me whinging about Glenn, while Dave plays therapist and talks me out of quitting the band. Now, even Adam's questioning why he's been forced into bass lessons while Glenn does whatever he wants. I've got no answer for him.

Since Glenn can't be trusted to stay sober before a show, we're discussing possibilities for a new singer. As for Derek, he's close to having outlived his usefulness. Tonight's episode is just another nail in his coffin. Steve's had enough of him claiming the bulk of our money for the phone bill.

It was important for all of us to put on a good show tonight. In the crowd were two film students from Ryerson University. They want to shoot a video for *Fantasy Merry-Go-Round*. Since we didn't get our FACTOR grant in September, this could be a good deal for us. As students, they've got access to professional gear and facilities at a fraction of the regular cost. They reckon they can deliver a $20,000 video for $2,000. And they're willing to split that cost down the middle with us.

We haven't left them with a great first impression.

Burned into my mind is Glenn, heavy-lidded, sweating and slurring his way through our set. At the end, he turns toward us, his face wet and beaming, and shouts, "Great show guys!"

"What the fuck is he talking about?" I think to myself.

Is he on drugs or something?

Why, yes.

Yes. He is.

TRANSCRIPT OF SNEAKY DEE'S SHOW

Friday, November 15, 1991

Introduction

Glenn:
Hey. Don't give me that look.

Steve Wright:
You mean the one of exasperation? That I seem to have on my face all too frequently?

Glenn:
What's exasperation?

(Steve Closs cuts in with guitar strum and feedback)

Steve Wright:
That was our first song. Thank you, goodnight.

Glenn:
That was Steve Closs on guitar.

Steve Wright:
(Pissed off) What the hell are we doing up here?

Steve Closs:
Better make a run for it . . .

(More guitar chords)

Steve Wright:
Good evening . . . Welcome to the SkyDome.

Glenn:
Close, that's just down the road.

Steve Closs:
Never mind the introduction, let's just play. We're the Marvelous Beauhunks from . . . that way . . . somewhere . . .

Steve Wright:
Off stage.

Glenn:
You don't wanna know where we're from.

Total—on stage for 1 minute 42 seconds before playing a song

1. Think it Over

Glenn:
Thank you.

Steve Closs:
Thank you.

Steve Closs:
I'd like to thank the few people who . . . whoa, there is people out there . . . OK . . . the many people who showed up today.

(Tunes guitar—ping ping)

Glenn:
Nuthin' else to do . . . come see the Beauhunks. This next song we're gonna do for you, is called . . . Tell You No Lies.

Total—32 seconds between songs

2. TYNL

Glenn:
Thank you!

Steve Closs:
That old tuning thing. Talk to the people Glenn.

(Steve Wright is about to count in the next song)

Glenn:
No. We're gonna do a little bit of the tuning of the guitar here . . .

(Steve Closs tunes . . . ping ping)

Glenn:
So, I think I'll have myself a drink.

Steve Wright:
Oh. Go figure.

Adam:
What a surprise.

Glenn:
So, what're ya saying?

Steve Wright:
I'm not saying anything, Glenn.

Glenn:
I guess whilst we're doing this, I'd like to thank the Coles for having us out here tonight.

Steve Wright:
And the Snow Dogs, whom we just met. They've been like father figures to us.

Glenn:
Great guys.

Steve Closs:
They're not even out there Steve.

Steve Wright:
Oh! They're not even here?

(Steve Wright counts in)

Total—54 seconds between songs

3. A Wish Away

Glenn:
Whoooo . . . . Thank you.

Steve Closs:
Thank you.

Glenn:
Oh! We're not going to tune again are we? OK. I guess we'll go on.

(Steve Wright counts in)

Total—20 seconds between songs

4. City Asleep

Glenn:
Thank you.

Steve Wright:
We really like this crowd up front here.

Glenn:
Get some more beer in ya!

Steve Closs:
Not to ruin the image of the band, this is straight vodka.

Glenn:
(laughs) And he's not joking.

Glenn:
K! I'm gonna get this right this time. This next song we're gonna do is . . . uh . . . probably . . . I dunno . . . probably my most favourite song of this set. Not that you care. Actually, I'm just killing time because he's tuning. So, bear with us.

(Steve Closs tunes . . . ping ping)

Glenn:
And that's it.

Glenn:
This is called . . . My Biggest . . . Thrill.

(Steve Wright counts in)

Total—54 seconds between songs

5. My Biggest Thrill

Glenn:
Thank you.

Steve Closs:
Thank you.

Total—20 seconds between songs

6. Coming Down

Steve Closs:
Thank you.

Steve Closs:
Somebody came up to me and said, "That song's about a big drug trip because it's coming down and colours and everything." And I said, "No mom, it's not, it's . . . uh . . . completely different."

Steve Wright:
That's when she was asking you what you were doing with your allowance.

Glenn:
Spending it on cocaine. It's only four dollars mum.

Glenn:
We're gonna take you back a few years.

(Steve Closs plays guitar intro)

Total—23 seconds between songs

7. Pressure Drop

Glenn:
Thank you.

Steve Closs:
Thank you. Sorry about the shade exit there.

Glenn:
We'll keep you in that ska mode for three and a half more minutes.

Steve Closs:
Can I switch my guitar yet? No?

Glenn:
This is called Two Swords.

(Steve Closs plays guitar intro)

Total—26 seconds between songs

8. Two Swords

Steve Closs:
Thank you.

Steve Closs:
Now, can I switch my guitar over?

(Closs switches guitars)

Glenn:
Now, we gotta switch guitars first . . .

Steve Wright:
We need about two minutes of dead silence.

Glenn:
Did everyone vote for that lady who . . . uh . . .

Steve Wright:
What's the difference between snot and broccoli? (Adam plays Barney Miller theme in background). Little kids won't eat broccoli.

(smattering of laughs and groans)

Steve Wright:
That was the only non-sexist thing I could think of to say. We got a little bad press up in the Peterborough area. Anybody here from Peterborough? Not you . . .

Steve Wright:
Anybody who finds anything offensive about our show, please leave now.

Glenn:
They think our name is very sexist—Marvelous Beauhunks, so we have a ballot box back here if anyone wants to leave any comments. Just give them to the drummer.

Steve Wright:
We'll just rip them up later.

Glenn:
OK.

Steve Wright:
We are the Coles.

Glenn:
This is for all of you idle people who love to sit around all day and watch soap operas. It's called *Kickin' Around.*

(Adam plays bass intro)

Total—33 seconds between songs

9. Kickin' Around

(Glenn forgets the words—there's only two verses in the whole song)

Glenn:
Thank you.

Steve Wright:
(to sound man) Can I get some of the bass down in the mix up here?

Glenn:
OK. This is . . . uh . . . this next song we're gonna do is kind of sad but true.

Steve Closs:
(sings) Here's a story sad but true. I know that one.

Glenn:
We're gonna slow it down a little bit . . . heh heh heh heh . . .

Glenn:
We're still doing that tuning thing.

Glenn:
It's called Pictures and Tears.

Total—39 seconds between songs

10, Pictures and Tears

Steve Closs:
Thank you.

Glenn:
Thank you.

(I start the next song without giving anyone a chance to tune up or fuck around . . . drums and bass start to cruise)

Steve Closs:
Now, if anyone didn't know anything else we played, if you don't know this one, we might as well get off now.

Glenn:
This next song hopefully is going to be a video in January. This one's for our video friends. They're in the audience somewhere.

Total—3 seconds between songs

11. Fantasy Merry—Go-Round

Glenn:
Thank you very much.

Steve Closs:
Thank you.

Glenn:
The dancing Coles.

Steve Closs:
Ladies and gentlemen . . . the Coles.

Glenn:
OK. This will be the last song for tonight . . . for us anyways.

Steve Wright:
So don't say anything bad about the Coles, we wouldn't want to make the Coles sore. (No one gets the pun but Adam)

Glenn:
This one's a little bit of a hopper.

(Steve starts Little Bitch intro)

Total—20 seconds between songs

<u>12. Little Bitch</u>

(Glenn turns to us and says, "Great show guys!")

REHEARSAL

Tuesday, November 19, 1991

We laid down the law.

If Glenn wants to stay in the band, he'll have to stay sober before all shows. And he goes to vocal lessons.

This is our careers on the line. If he's not on board, we're prepared to find someone who is.

Welcome to MARVELOUS BEAUHUNKS® INC.

Glenn's contrite and apologetic. He seems sincere and it's hard to stay mad at him.

But then again, Glenn has a habit of telling you what you want to hear.

LARGESS FOR LADIES

NOW Magazine, Thursday, November 28, 1991
By Kim Hughes

*Toronto's Barenaked Ladies have been awarded an impressive $100,000 from radio station CFNY as part of their "Discovery to Disk" program—something CFNY director of programming and operations **Reiner Schwarz** calls "a kind of unspoken tax or provision, giving something back," in compliance with CRTC licensing regulations.*

On the flip side, Schwarz allows that CFNY is awarded "exclusive rights to air the material before it's released, either in feature shows or rotation. But it's not an album for exclusive play on CFNY." Nor will any song be played without the band's consent.

*"It's a thrill for the station to offer that much money to the band in the first place," says Ladies manager **Nigel Best**. "Then for them to point the finger at us is so great. It's such a pat on the back."*

*Just a reminder that the Ladies and guests the Waltons play the **Music Hall** November 29 and 30 (sold out) as well as the CASBYs and the Toronto Music Awards, happening December 1 and 4 respectively. The Ladies are nominated for awards in both camps.*

CLINTON'S, TORONTO—w/ SKAFACE

Friday, November 29, 1991

This is our first time at Clinton's. The soundman tells us that he was the touring sax player for the Diodes. He claims to be the one who came up with the title *Tired of Waking Up Tired* while driving the van. According to him, they never even gave him a writing credit.

Okay.

Between songs, Steve announces that he'd like to dedicate the next number to Freddie Mercury, who died this past Sunday. Adam chimes into the mike "looks like another one bites the dust," and makes a *whoomp-whoomp* sound on his bass.

Steve is shooting daggers at Adam while the club sits in stunned silence. Adam doesn't realize that the crowd basically just heard him say "another fag dies of AIDS."

We're already the sexist band from Oshawa. I guess we might as well be the homophobic one too.

Nice one, Adam.

NEIGHBOURS

December 1, 1991

Richard's moved out of the main floor of seven-eighty-two. He's been great, giving us access to the basement all year. We're going to miss him.

Now, Glenn and Davy are our neighbours. The cost of the rehearsal space just went through the roof. The price—my sanity. Once upon a time, the night was peaceful and silent. Now there's constant music, parties and a revolving door of people.

As I lay in bed staring at the ceiling, the music finally stops. I start to drift off into a hard-won slumber.

Bzzzzzzz . . . Bzzzzzzz . . . Bzzzzzzz . . . Bzzzzzzz . . .

Christ.

I roll out of bed, bleary-eyed.

Time for work.

My shift starts at 7 a.m. Glenn doesn't start work until 2:30 this afternoon. Like clockwork, he'll call in sick. I'll hear no end of it from the store manager.

As I get ready to leave, I grab my keys from the kitchen table. Adam's door is open. His bed is empty. He must be at Lisa's. I pick up *In The City* by the Jam and stick it in the CD player. In retaliation, I turn the volume up to full, head down the stairs and out the door.

Fucking nuisance.

FANTASY MERRY-GO-ROUND—FINAL MUSIC VIDEO PROPOSAL (Page 1)

December 1991

Visual Concept

We start with extreme close-ups of a circa-1960 record player as a record drops and begins to spin. The arm swings over and rests on the disc. Scratches are heard . . . and then the music starts.

Cut to the band playing in a warehouse as the camera circles around them. Movements are faster than normal, yet in synch with the music. The camera movement is unrestrained, with the images becoming blurred at times.

At times, we cut away to the band in a more candid, "home movie-ish" atmosphere. This would be filmed in the band's home and around Oshawa. Documentary-like, irregular camera movement with harsh zooms, slow motion and erratic sungun lighting.

We will occasionally cut back to tactile close-ups of the record player. Particular emphasis is paid to the turntable, speaker fabric, needle, grooves of the record itself, etc.

As the song ends, we cut from the performance back to the record player as the needle lifts and returns to its original position.

The overall look will be black and white with varying degrees of high contrast and coarse grain. A slight tint may also be added to the image.

Grand total $2,335.

FANTASY MERRY-GO-ROUND—FINAL MUSIC VIDEO PROPOSAL (Page 2)

December 1991

Production Schedule

Development: *(November 1 to November 30, 1991)*

- *Written proposal*
- *Working concepts*
- *Band consultation*
- *Final concept*
- *Cutting a deal*

Pre-production: *(December 1, 1991 to January 10, 1992)*

- *Camera tests*
- *Location scouting*
- *Equipment booking*
- *Crew assembly*
- *Filming permits*
- *Final production schedule*

Production—Principal photography

- *Friday, January 17, 1992*
- *Saturday, January 18, 1992*
- *Sunday, January 19, 1992*

Post-production: *(February 1 to February 28, 1992)*

- *Film processing*
- *Film transfer to video*
- *Video editing*
- *Final cut*
- *Final payment*

Completed video: *(February 29, 1992)*

Dave Kazala

Michael Wale

BRAMCHESTER BEAT—CFNY XMAS PARTY

Wednesday, December 4, 1991

We're back on the upswing. CFNY is planning its big, end-of-year blowout and we're second on the bill.

December 18th will see us playing the Phoenix Concert Theatre as part of the *Bramchester Beat, CFNY Xmas Party* with SKAFACE, the Coles and I.C.E.

Not long ago, the Phoenix was the Diamond. In 1989, Adam and I watched Steve Jones from the Sex Pistols open for Ian Hunter and Mick Ronson. Before that, I had one of my best dates there, seeing the Stray Cats.

I expect this show will be on the level of our live recording at UltraSound back in August. High profile. Lots of fanfare. It's our much-needed second chance. And, this time, we're ready for it.

Musically, the band has gone through its "Hamburg" period. Over the last few months, Adam's become a competent and knowledgeable bass-player. Both Steve's guitar-chops and his ego have grown at an exponential rate. Even my game has been raised, with my playing becoming less chaotic and more solid.

We're also paying more attention to the visual aspect of our show. Three button jackets are appearing on stage. Compulsive tunings between songs are decreasing. We're starting to earn the attention that we've been getting for free.

The Marvelous Beauhunks are a more mature band. I want to lose our teeny-bopper appeal and come across as more well-heeled and mod.

More Weller—less *Well, d'uh . . .*

This is our time.

HOW THE BARENAKED LADIES STOLE XMAS

NOW Magazine—Thursday December 5, 1991

Thursday, December 19, 1991
MCA Concerts and CFNY FM 102.1 Present

BARENAKED CIRCUS '91

FEATURING:
ANDREW CASH, SKYDIGGERS, BARENAKED LADIES, MOXY FRUVOUS, CORKY & THE JUICEPIGS, MADAME BUSKERFLY & MORE

PHOENIX CONCERT THEATRE

Tickets $2.00 @Ticketmaster (No Service Charge)
All Proceeds to Daily Bread Food Bank
Admission Only By Ticket With Non-Perishable Food Items
*Doors Open @ 7:00 PM * 19 Yrs & Older*

HOW THE BARENAKED LADIES STOLE XMAS

The Barenaked Ladies are booked at the Phoenix the night after us?

Ever since that ad came out in NOW Magazine for the *Barenaked Circus '91*, there's been no promotion for the *Bramchester Beat, CFNY Xmas Party*.

No radio plugs, nothing in print.

We're CFNY's forgotten, second-stringers.

If you have a problem, and if you can find them, maybe you can hire . . . The B-Team.

The CFNY landscape is changing and it appears that the Marvelous Beauhunks are no more than bit-players.

Fuck.

CELEBRATE CHRISTMAS WITH THE BEAUHUNKS

Friday, December 6, 1991

The Marvelous Beauhunks are preparing for another major show in Toronto.

The Oshawa band will play at the Phoenix Concert Theatre (formerly the Diamond), on Sherbourne Street, on December 18 as part of the CFNY Christmas Showcase. Toronto bands Skaface, the Coles, and I.C.E. will also perform.

Admission to the concert is $5 at the door or $3 in advance.

SILVER DOLLAR, TORONTO—w/ Genetic Rhythm

Friday, December 6, 1991

I'm down with a nasty chest-cold. My lungs are congested and I've got a throat-shredding cough to match. It's with no small effort that I've managed to crawl out of bed. Adam's driving my car so I can rest up on our way to the gig.

The sky is pitch black when we pull into the gas station to fuel up. Ever the mechanic, Adam checks the oil levels and decides that my car needs a quart. While the hood's up, I sit quietly in the passenger seat and watch light, fluffy snowflakes fall under the neon lights.

Adam opens the driver-side door and gets in.

"Sorry, man. I accidentally put a litre of oil into your windshield-wiper reservoir," he says.

In my weakened state I'm too tired to care. We take the Ritson Road onramp toward Toronto and wait for the heater to warm up.

At the Silver Dollar, we meet the band that we're sharing the stage with. They're friendly kids from Brampton and the band's called Genetic Rhythm. The singer's got a powerful voice and a Bowie fixation. In comparison, Glenn's voice is thin and two-dimensional.

He's still not going to his vocal lessons.

I summon the energy to play my drums, and we live to fight another day.

Saturday, December 7, 1991

I called in sick to work. That didn't stop Maria and I from going to see the Waltons, at UltraSound.

After they finished their set, I went up to the Waltons' bass-player and introduced myself.

"Hi. I'm Steve Wright. I'm the drummer for the Marvelous Beauhunks. Good gig tonight. We should book a show together sometime," I said.

"I know who you are," the Waltons' bass-player replied.

Then he turned his back and walked away.

PSYCHEDELIC FURS

Sunday, December 15, 1991

"This is the fourth time someone from your organization has called us about this. Don't call again. We'll call you if we want you."

The Psychedelic Furs are playing RPM on December 15th. The promoters are the Gary's and CPI.

We told Derek that we want this gig. His calls aren't being returned. Adam phoned the promoters and said that he was taking over management for the band. They told him not to call back.

Steve's sure it's because we tanked the Transvision Vamp show.

I don't know what to think other than Derek's not getting the job done.

A BEAUHUNKS KIND OF CHRISTMAS

Oshawa/Whitby This Week, Wednesday, December 18, 1991

Popular Oshawa-based band the Marvelous Beauhunks take the stage at Pizza Pino's for a pre-Christmas concert in Ajax this Saturday.

The all-ages event features a guest performance by the Mindset. Tickets are available at the door.

CFNY PRESENTS THE BRAMCHESTER BEAT XMAS PARTY (PART 1)

Wednesday, December 18, 1991

I'm still laid up with the same chest-cold from a few weeks ago. No matter what I do, I can't shake it. I'm a sweaty, snotty mess.

We're expected to be at the Phoenix ridiculously early for sound-check. I'd rather be doing anything else, but the show must go on.

Maria's asked if we can stop by her classroom on the way downtown. She wants us to do an impromptu performance for her fourth-graders. Surprisingly, the other guys are going along with it.

We bring in the amps and set them low. I play my snare drum with brushes, while Glenn bangs a tambourine and sings like he's already at the Phoenix.

These kids have never heard of us before today. Because we're on the radio, they think they're in the presence of rock-and-roll royalty. After a few songs, we open the floor to some Q&A.

"What did you do before you were rock stars?"

"What do you do when you're not being rock stars?"

We pack the gear, sign some autographs, and hit the road like we're the Rolling Stones on tour.

The kids are over the moon and the old lady's happy.

CFNY PRESENTS THE BRAMCHESTER BEAT XMAS PARTY (PART 2)

Wednesday, December 18, 1991

My clothes are soaked through. I can't stop sweating. The stage and the PA are the best we've ever played on. The engineer tells us that we sound good, so we finish up our sound-check.

CFNY's laid out a big pizza spread for all the bands to share. Adam refuses to eat it.

"I don't know where all these other bands have been," he sniffs.

It's his turn to throw the latest fit.

I could care less. I have no appetite.

We leave Steve and Glenn to their pizza and we find a cheap chicken dinner down the street.

CFNY PRESENTS THE BRAMCHESTER BEAT XMAS PARTY (PART 3)

Wednesday, December 18, 1991

We're watching I.C.E. on the stage. They're first in tonight's line-up.

I notice that their drummer has the same snare drum as me. I look more closely. He's got the same seat, cymbals and stands as me.

The fucking twat is using my gear.

He's taken all the equipment that I carefully positioned during sound-check and changed it around to suit himself. And now he's using it onstage.

As soon as the last note of their set is in the air, I'm right up in his business. I tell him to keep his fucking grubby mitts off my gear.

He's all, "What's your problem, ma-aan?"

You're my fucking problem, you grabby prick.

Don't touch my fucking stuff again or I'll smash your face in.

Asshole.

CFNY PRESENTS THE BRAMCHESTER BEAT XMAS PARTY (PART 4)

Wednesday, December 18, 1991

We're backstage when Hal Harbour drops in. We haven't seen much of him since the live recording at UltraSound. He's emcee for tonight's show.

While the Coles play their set, we ask Hal what he's been up to. He's been in Halifax, for the East Coast Music Awards. With him is a cassette from one of the best new bands he's ever seen.

We try to appear enthusiastic as Hal tells us about this great new group. In reality, our hearts are sinking. It feels like Hal's breaking up with us.

This new band to watch out for is called Sloan.

CFNY PRESENTS THE BRAMCHESTER BEAT XMAS PARTY (PART 5)

Wednesday, December 18, 1991

The Barenaked Ladies have indeed stolen Christmas from us.

As feared, the Phoenix is only half-full. Even Steve and Damyana's cart-them-in-by-bus strategy hasn't been able to attract enough punters to get us near capacity. Regardless of our disappointment, we've got a job to do.

It's time to pay the rent.

We start the show with *Think It Over*. Steve strums a walloping E chord and sings the first note. They don't match. His voice cracks as he awkwardly stretches the bum note into the right key. With that as our introduction, the chequered flag is dropped.

Our recovery is quick and, soon, we're racing in top form. New original songs, like *Same Old Story* and *Remains to be Scene*, fit nicely amongst the English Beat covers that we've recently added to the set. The coolness of the psychedelic-tinged *Coming Down* helps to cancel out the silliness of the insipid *Coffee-Maker*.

As we roar into the final lap, we hit the nitrous and shift into high-energy overdrive with *Like Wow—Wipeout*. Steve and Adam crouch on the drum-riser, heads down, jousting with their guitar necks. As the song reaches its thunderous climax, they leap simultaneously from the riser, into the air.

My fever is broken.

CFNY PRESENTS THE BRAMCHESTER BEAT XMAS PARTY (PART 6)

Wednesday, December 18, 1991

Backstage, Derek congratulates us for pulling off a truly raucous show. In the audience are the two singers and manager of the accursed Barenaked Ladies. According to Derek, they like the band. I think Derek's being diplomatic.

Either way, I think the Barenaked Ladies suck.

Maria's waiting for me by the bar. She's brought a group of her college-rock-poseur friends with her to the show. I can barely stomach them. One of her old university roommates is here to pass judgement on me. We've never met before tonight. Apparently, if you don't pass muster with her, then you don't last as Maria's boyfriend.

Instead of letting things escalate into a battle of the giants, I head the ex-roommate off at the pass. I greet her with a big hug and a warm hello. At least on the surface, I'm given the seal of approval.

I don't know who this chick is or why she thinks it's her job to judge me, but, from where I stand, she can slurp my butt.

I hate Maria's friends.

EYE WEEKLY—The 1991 OK? Handy Dandy Chart

Thursday, December 19, 1991

Best Local Act

1. *Infidels, P.S.*
2. *Courage of Lassie, J.A.*
3. *Dream Warriors, C.OC.*
4. *Sara Craig, C.J.*
5. *Sara Craig, B.R.*

Worst Local Act

6. *Pure, P.S.*
7. *Nancy Sinatras, J.A.*
8. ***The Marvelous Beauhunks, C.OC.***
9. *Holly Cole Trio, C.J.*
10. *Tom "Metaphor" Cochrane, B.R*

LOST IN THE SUPERMARKET

Thursday, December 19, 1991

"Have you seen the latest issue of EYE?" Derek asks me, while I load more iceberg lettuce onto the wet-counter.

"Nooo . . ." I say impatiently, waiting for the punch line.

"C.J. O'Connor voted us one of the top five worst bands in Toronto! You can't buy publicity like this!"

Derek's typically enthusiastic. He thinks this is great news.

I don't think this is great news at all. In fact it's terrible news. It confirms what I've known all along. That we're not as good as people think we are.

Now here it is in black and white. Someone's finally seen through us. And he's called us out in a very public way.

"Think about it," Derek says.

"Look at who we're lumped in with. Tom Cochrane. Holly Cole. Pure. That's pretty fucking good company. You've got to see what a great opportunity this is for us."

I guess he makes sense. But it still doesn't make me feel any better.

This is bad.

Very bad.

REHEARSAL

Thursday, December 19, 1991

We're pretty down in the dumps.

As expected, Steve wants to go after C.J. O'Connor . . . *Beauhunk-style* . . . but we're really too bummed for much bravado.

We cut it short and call it a night.

NOW MAGAZINE—Top 10 Albums of 1991

Thursday, December 19, 1991

NOW Magazine's Top 10 Albums of 1991

#1—Nirvana—Nevermind

#2—Brand New Heavies—S/T

#3—Loreena McKennitt—The Visit

#4—Circle C—S/T

#5—Lenny Kravitz—Mama Said

#6—Sara Craig—S/T

#7—P.M. Dawn—Of The Heart, Of The Soul, And Of The Cross

#8—Texas—Mothers Heaven

#9—Pearl Jam—Ten

#10—Aster Aweke—Kabu

PIZZA PINO'S, AJAX—w/ The Mindset

Saturday, December 21, 1991

Where is everyone?

I thought for sure this place would be packed. That's the only reason we booked it.

Tonight's supposed to be an easy cash-grab to finance the cassette. Why else would we ever play Pizza Pino's again?

"People thought it was a goof," said the kid with the camera.

"Nobody actually believed you guys would play here. You're way bigger than this."

I thank the kid for saying so. In the back of my mind, I wonder if the article in EYE didn't have something to do with it. We should be walking away with at least $500. We'll be lucky to bring in $150.

The manager insists that we pay his girl to work the door for us. Steve tells him to forget it. Damyana's got her cashbox and she's handling our money.

We get down to it, play our two sets and we pack up. Before we leave, we take some pictures for the kid with the camera and a few of his friends. As we're heading for the door, the manager takes another run at Steve. He wants money for his girl.

"We're not paying her $20," Steve repeats.

"You'll never play here again," the manager hisses at Steve.

"Do you know who the fuck we are?" Steve laughs, his voice dripping condescension.

"We're the fucking Marvelous Beauhunks."

With those words of good cheer hanging in the air, we break for Christmas.

Nineteen-ninety-one ends in the exact same place that 1990 did.

All I can say is good-fucking-riddance.

CHRISTMAS MEMORIES FROM DURHAM'S MUSIC PEOPLE

Oshawa/Whitby This Week, Sunday Edition, Sunday, December 22, 1991
By John Duarte
This Week Entertainment Writer

Christmas music is guaranteed to get a reaction out of just about anyone. No matter what your musical tastes, Yuletide songs are enjoyed by everyone.

Some of the local music people have their favourites and here is a sampling of what they had to say:

*The **Marvelous Beauhunks** unanimously agree their favourite Christmas recording is any seasonal music by Elvis. After reading the list of remarkable facts Stephen Wright, Adam Graham, Stephen Closs and Glenn Goodman have discovered, you will likely rush out to buy a copy of your very own.*

The Beauhunks say: "Both Elvis and Santa are jolly, fat men; both have extremely well-groomed, stylish facial hair; Elvis and Santa Claus have never been photographed together; both have a notorious appetite for cookies, doughnuts and milk; Santa Claus lives in secluded splendour, surrounded by small friends and many toys; so does Elvis . . . no wait! That's Michael Jackson; when played backwards, the Elvis recording of Blue Christmas actually states, 'I am Santa Claus'."

Is there any question left in your mind? Elvis is Santa Claus!

. . .

We're down to having Adam go out and conduct interviews on his own.

As part of Oshawa's musical elite, our opinions about Christmas have been lumped in with the likes of Mike from Star Records and the guy from Harem Scarem.

Unbelievably, the manager from the Barenaked Ladies has crammed sentiments about missing children into the same sentence as "hip" Bing Crosby references.

Fuck me - are these guys always "on"?

Oy vey.

HEY AMIGO

Monday, December 30, 1991

Nineteen-ninety-two is about to be born under a bad sign.

Effective immediately, Adam's in charge of all Marvelous Beauhunks business.

His first task: Notify Derek that he's been made redundant.

Adam says it went like this:

"I knocked on the door and Derek invited me in. I told him his services as manager for the Marvelous Beauhunks were no longer required. Then I walked out."

That cold bastard's our new manager.

LEE'S PALACE, TORONTO—w/ SKAFACE, the Coles

Friday, January 3, 1992

Being the drummer in the Marvelous Beauhunks has become just another shitty job, except for the fact that it's also the most interesting thing about me.

Every conversation is something to do with the band. Friends. Family. Co-workers. Strangers. That's all they want to know about. I don't exist.

"How's the band?"

"What's the band up to?"

"When are you guys playing next?"

"I hear you're one of the top-five worst bands in Toronto."

Shoppers stare at me in the supermarket. I'm recognized in the streets. There goes one of the Marvelous Beauhunks.

"Hey Beauhunk!"

I put my head down and keep walking.

Glenn loves it, but I hate it. Fame sucks. And fame without money sucks balls.

Tonight, we're at Lee's Palace with SKAFACE and the Coles. I'm here to punch the clock at my shitty job. Since we're on first, I can go to bed early. No dragging my ass first thing in the morning.

Because I work hard at two shitty jobs.

I hate me.

You probably do too.

Saturday, January 4, 1992

Glenn called in sick to work again. He was supposed to start at 2:30 p.m. I've been here since 7:00 a.m.

I'm tired of the store manager giving me shit whenever Glenn doesn't show up.

Nothing to do with me, man.

You're the fucking guy that hired him.

CLINTON'S, TORONTO—Genetic Rhythm Video Release

Thursday, January 9, 1992

With Derek gone, we're a leaner unit. But something still feels off. It doesn't help that we sound-checked at 6:30 p.m. and we don't go on until 11 p.m. There's too much time to think.

Genetic Rhythm is a likeable group and their video for *Time is Perverse* has turned out well. I hope we're as lucky with our video.

The song is good too, except for that line about "time falling, wanking to the floor".

I know my Bowie and you're just not slipping that one past me.

Nice try though.

EPONYMOUS

Friday, January 10, 1992

Earlier in the day, with considerable effort, Adam lugged five heavy boxes marked *MBH-001* up the staircase of seven-eighty-two. He piled them on the kitchen floor, one on top of another, and left them there.

Now, we all stand together . . . *marvelling* . . . at their contents. Five hundred copies of the first EP from the Marvelous Beauhunks, released on our very own *782unes* record label.

We're legit now, fellas.

Well, maybe not completely legit. The cover of our cassette is almost certainly a violation of some copyright law, somewhere.

Because he could, Steve had vetoed all the creativity out of our album art.

We've got no title for the EP—Steve vetoed everyone's suggestions.

We've got no original artwork—Steve vetoed Wolfgang Mueller painting the cover in favour of having his brother do it.

Except Steve didn't follow-through.

No cover art was produced.

Just before we hit the deadline to go into production, I sat at the kitchen table with scissors, *Letraset*, and a picture of Pete Townsend from my *The Kids Are Alright* album.

I covered Pete's head with the band's logo.

Hopefully, people will think it's Steve.

All things considered, it's come out looking pretty cool.

VIDEO PRODUCTION (PRINCIPAL PHOTOGRAPHY)

Friday, January 17, 1992

"OK! Let's wrap it up for today. Good job everyone."

We've just finished 10 hours of start and stop filming at the abandoned Gooderham and Worts warehouse in Toronto. I'm more than ready to go home. After loading the truck, Adam directs us onto the Gardiner Expressway toward the Don Valley. We slowly battle the traffic back to Oshawa. It's dark outside. It was dark when we got here too.

I had no idea how tedious filming a video could be. Wide shots. Close-ups. Reaction shots. Lighting changes. Camera angles. Every change meant we had to play along to *Fantasy Merry-Go-Round* at half-speed, while someone slowly pushed the cameraman around on a circular dolly. Every time the camera focused on a new person, we'd have to mime our way through the song all over again.

Cut. Let's take it from the top. Remember to look energetic!

Around and around and around . . .

Again and again and again . . .

Tomorrow, Mike and Dave will come out to Oshawa to film us at seven-eighty-two and down at the pier.

They figure, they can get all the footage they need in one day. That'll cut Sunday off the shooting schedule.

Thank the Lord.

I'm beginning to hate that fucking song.

(Photo—Trish Mennell)

VIDEO PRODUCTION (PRINCIPAL PHOTOGRAPHY)

Saturday, January 18, 1992

Glenn's standing on the edge of the Oshawa pier with a life preserver around his neck. I'm holding onto the rope that's hanging from it. The temperature is so low today that the lake is actually warmer than the air outside. Clouds of steam are rising off the water. In the background, Adam laughs and smokes a cigarette.

All of this is being captured by Mike and Dave on a Super 8 handheld camera. They direct the four of us to walk around in the snow. It's a sunny January day, but the high-velocity wind and the icy cold make it almost unbearable. None of us are wearing hats or gloves. We're going to have to get the external shots done quickly.

We joke around and try to look like we're a cohesive, functioning band.

Try to look like you like each other . . .

Before long, Mike and Dave have what they need. They'll splice the outdoor footage with the "candid" shots they took back at seven-eighty-two.

We pile into the back of the white, rented, cargo van and we're dropped at home.

All that's left to do is wait for the finished product.

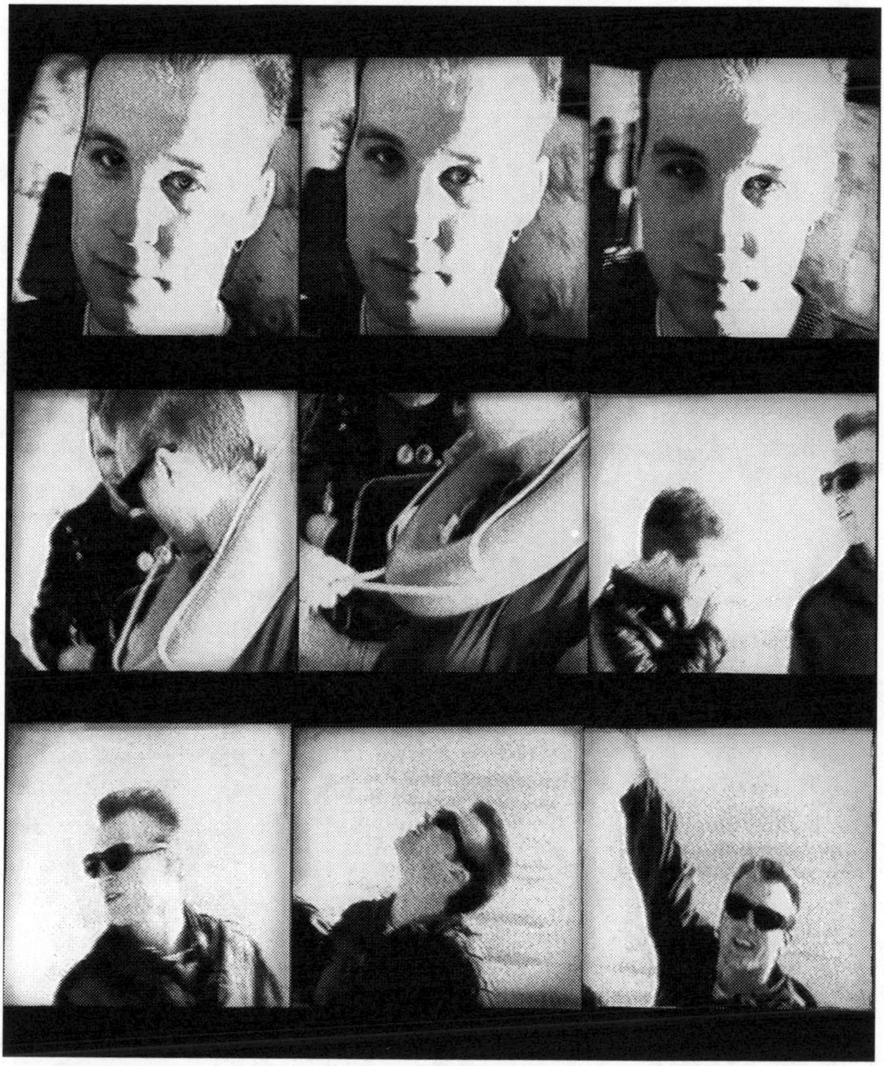

(Photo—Trish Mennell)

OSHAWA'S BEAUHUNKS GO ON THE RECORD

Oshawa/Whitby This Week, Weekend Edition, Sunday, January 19, 1992

Oshawa's own Marvelous Beauhunks are inviting local fans to the group's record release party at UltraSound, in Toronto, on February 1.

The band's first independent cassette will be released on the 782unes Music label. The release will feature six original songs including Fantasy Merry-Go-Round, which made it into the top 30 at Brampton FM station CFNY.

The band devoted its first year to writing original material. In May, Fantasy Merry-Go-Round appeared on the CFNY modern music compilation release. The song became a favourite of the station's listeners and climbed to number 16 on CFNY's weekly music chart, the highest position reached by any song on the Modern Music compilation compact disc. All songs on the Beauhunks' debut cassette were written and recorded between November 1990 and August 1991 at White Room Studios in Whitby. The cassette will be available at selected music stores in the area and at band performances. This is the only record release party the band will host, so fans are advised to be on hand.

OSHAWA'S BEAUHUNKS ARE SIMPLY MARVELOUS

The Chronicle, January 21, 1992
By Mike Campbell, Chronicle Staff

One of Oshawa's most promising new bands, the Marvelous Beauhunks, will be releasing their debut cassette in January.

The band was formed by guitarist Stephen Closs and drummer Stephen Wright. After playing together for several years, and various bands, bassist Adam Graham and lead vocalist Glenn Goodman were recruited.

Although they are all from various bands this "is their first attempt at a musical career," said Adam. "The other bands were nothing to the extent of what we are doing now."

Their demonstration tape, which is composed of six original songs, was made in the White Room in Whitby.

"The White Room is a 16-track studio, but it sounds like a 24-track," said Adam.

The self-produced release is a 60's sounding, British Invasion influenced tape with a 90's touch to it.

One song on the tape, "Fantasy Merry-Go-Round", appeared on the CFNY 1991 Modern Music compilation.

The song eventually reached number 16 on the station's weekly top 30 singles countdown.

The video for the song will be released on February 29.

The black-and-white half performance, half concept video was shot in Oshawa and Toronto.

A cassette release party will be held on Saturday, February 1, at UltraSound in Toronto.

NEW CANADIAN
BANDSTAND
PRESENTS
The
Marvelous
BeauHunks
with special guests
ONE WORD;
GOTTSCHLEIM
Purple
ONION
wed feb 12
"tape release
party"
22 Athol Street E., Oshawa, Ontario 576-9898

Wednesday, January 22, 1992

Before we sacked him, Derek left us with a packed schedule to play out. It'll be a while before Adam even needs to think about filling the calendar.

One of the dates Derek booked was Wednesday, February 12th, at the Purple Onion.

This would be the same Purple Onion whose manager didn't think we were good enough to open for the pseudo-Byrds. I guess he's changed his mind. Even though it's close to home, I could give two shits about playing his club. Still, it'll be more effort to fight with the other guys than to actually play the gig.

I let it slide.

That is until Adam brings home the flyer the Purple Onion is using to promote the show. Along the bottom, in happy letters, it says "*tape release party.*"

Why do people keep doing this to me?

We're not having any "tape release party" on Wednesday, February 12th. Certainly not in Oshawa, and certainly not at the Purple Onion. We're having one, and only one, cassette release and it's at UltraSound on Saturday, February 1st.

We've put ourselves on the line by guaranteeing Yvonne that we can fill UltraSound on a Saturday night. If we don't, we're not likely to get a second chance anytime soon. The last thing we need is the Purple Onion undercutting our efforts to make good on our promise to Yvonne.

I'm in full-on confrontation mode. I tell Adam I'll handle it.

At high-noon, I walk out of a cold winter sun into the dimly lit Purple Onion. I look hard into the eyes of the greeter at the door. The promotions girl is summoned. When she appears, I thrust the poster into her hand.

"What the hell is this?" I demand.

She looks at the poster and she looks at me. She looks at the poster again. She's got no idea who I am.

"I'm the drummer for the Marvelous Beauhunks and we're NOT having a 'TAPE RELEASE PARTY' here," I announce with smug authority.

"I want every poster around town, taken down immediately."

The promotions girl apologizes, and tells me she'll do her best. I advise her that she'd better.

The Marvelous Beauhunks are professionals. We don't put up with this kind of bush-league tomfoolery.

Holstering my ego, I drive back to seven-eighty-two and tell Adam that the problem's been solved.

Beauhunk-style . . .

Thursday, January 23, 1992

On my way home from work, I stopped at the library to check out a book about depression and anxiety disorders. For months, I've felt that something's becoming very wrong with me.

My chest is always tight, I'm constantly angry and I generally want to throw up. Just leaving the house has become a difficult chore.

I go through the checklist for anxiety disorders and panic attacks.

Heart palpitations—Yup

Muscle weakness and tension—Yes

Fatigue—Yes

Nausea—Uh huh

Chest pain—Check

Shortness of breath—Got it

Stomach aches—Yes

Headaches—Yup

Sense of dread or panic—Definitely

Feeling as if I will pass out—Uh huh

Feelings of apprehension or dread—Yes

Trouble concentrating—What was I just doing . . . . ?

Tense or jumpy—Yup

Anticipating the worst—Always

Irritability—Oh yeah

Restlessness—Yes

Watching and waiting for signs and occurrences of danger—Constantly

Now that I know what to look for, I'll work extra hard to hide it.

As far as anybody else needs to know, everything's just fine.

Friday, January 24, 1992

Glenn and I are postering Queen Street in the middle of a blizzard. Glenn never gets his hands dirty when it's time to hang flyers. Because of that, Adam put his foot down on principle and has refused to help. This would've been a good day for me to put my foot down too. It's a mess out here.

We stop by UltraSound, to get out of the grey skies and blinding snow, and check in with Yvonne. She gives us a warm greeting and she's pleased to hear about the promotion we've been doing for the show. Adam's got press-releases out to any paper who'd take them, Steve and Damyana have a bus-package organized, and we're playing live on Citytv's Breakfast Television, Tuesday morning.

We're ultra-confident that we'll pack UltraSound.

Take that Purple Onion.

BREAKFAST TELEVISION (Citytv), TORONTO

Tuesday, January 28, 1992

We cut back in from commercial. Ann Rohmer, host of *Citytv's Breakfast Television*, steps up to introduce us.

"Marvelous Beauhunks . . . that's what they call themselves. So if we widen out, we'll see why. They have a cassette release party at UltraSound Showbar on Saturday. It's called 'the Marvelous Beauhunks' and here they are with . . . what's it called? . . . Fantasy Merry-Go-Round . . . I knew that."

I'm miserable.

Three-thirty in the morning is an ugly time to get out of bed on any day. It's especially hard in the freezing cold of January. Acidic stomachs meet with the crunchy sound of snowy footsteps. Small sounds echo eerily in a dark and empty neighbourhood, while streetlamps provide just enough florescent light to keep your balance.

There's nowhere open to get coffee, so cigarettes will have to make due for the trip down the Don Valley Parkway. By 5 a.m., we've arrived at Queen and John and are loading the equipment onto the studio floor. Once we're all set-up, we'll sound check and wait for ten-to-eight when we make our first appearance on live television.

My anxiety levels are peaking. I'm starting to become unglued. Every day sees me huddled around the toilet, gagging and retching in secret. I don't know how much longer I can hide it. I feel exposed. People are looking at me and whispering behind my back. Spiders are laying eggs in my brain. I can't picture a future where I'm dependent on the actions of Steve and Glenn. The idea of touring across Canada with them, in a smelly cargo van, is unfathomable.

Even Maria and her family, all wonderful people, make me feel bad. They like me a lot and I keep waiting for them to realize that I'm a worthless and horrible person. If I relax and let my defences down for even a second, all of my bad thoughts will come true. I replay all potential scenarios in my mind so I can stay prepared.

The song is over.

Ann steps out in front of the band and addresses the camera.

"Big finish . . . big finish. It's the Marvelous Beauhunks. I have five passes for Lawrence of Arabia at the Ontario Place Cinesphere on February 2nd, if you can tell me where the Marvelous Beauhunks are performing on February 1st. The first five callers at eight-seven-oh, seven-seven-one-six will win.

Right now we're going into the CityPulse newsroom to take a look at traffic . . ."

We've got nothing to do until our next performance, when we play out the credits at five-minutes-to-nine. A production assistant takes us on a tour of Citytv and we see the offices where the writers work. We're shown the MuchMusic studio. It's tiny compared to how it looks on television.

Ann Rohmer stops to visit with us for a moment. She says to Glenn and me, "You look like Jim Morrison without hair." And she walks away.

Glenn insists that she was talking to him. I insist that she was talking to me. We argue about it. Intent on settling the debate, I catch up to Ann and ask her who she thinks looks like "Jim Morrison without hair."

"You both do," she replies without missing a beat, as she strides away.

We sit in the audience chairs and watch quietly, as they continue to broadcast the show. Glancing at Steve, I notice how haggard he looks. His dad's in the hospital with terminal cancer. Steve spends every night by his side until the small hours of the morning. To cover the bags and dark circles under his eyes, Steve's been wearing a pair of John Lennon-style sunglasses when on camera.

Daylight's beginning to flood Queen Street and it's time for us to play again. We wrap our appearance with *Pictures and Tears*, pack up our gear and go our separate ways.

Adam and I get into the truck and head east on Queen Street.

"I'm never doing that again," I tell him.

Adam shrugs.

He knows I speak the truth.

TALE OF THE TAPE

Oshawa-Whitby This Week, Wednesday, Jan. 29, 1992
John Duarte, This Week Entertainment Writer

The Marvelous Beauhunks have come a long way in one year.

Last spring the band was about to call it quits when the first gig came along. Soon after that, Brampton radio station CFNY-FM placed the group's entry in the Modern Music contest on the compilation compact disc showcasing the best entries in the contest.

"We were very lucky," said bass player Adam Graham last summer, just as the band was beginning to turn heads on the club circuit in Toronto.

But luck is only partially responsible for the band's success. Graham and his band mates (Stephen Closs on guitar, lead vocalist Glenn Goodman, and drummer Stephen Wright) were persistent in their quest to get their name known on the club circuit and work toward recording their original material.

. . .

Now that the Marvelous Beauhunks have their first release available, the band can start looking ahead. As Graham says the group has set some short range goals ("doing the video is the next goal" and "selling every one of these tapes") and would like to land a recording deal with a major label, but nothing is etched in concrete.

"Of course, you have to set musical goals," Graham says. "Motivation is very important and keeping a proper perspective on the business."

The Beauhunks have managed to keep their music affairs balanced.

"We've been pretty successful in separating the business from the music in the music business," says Graham. "We have time that we take care of business and we have time that is strictly band time."

. . .

If only people knew what was happening behind the scenes. The other guys may not want to accept it, but it's only a matter of time before I'm gone.

I don't know how much longer I can hold on.

Wednesday, January 29, 1992

The Oshawa Times is sending someone to interview us tonight. I can't be bothered to get dressed. I put on my bathrobe and head down to the basement.

At seven o'clock, the interviewer arrives. I can hear Adam answering the door and leading him upstairs. I sit on my drum-stool, unwilling to move until I absolutely have to.

Eventually Glenn comes downstairs to collect me.

"What the fuck are you doing?" he asks. "We're waiting for you."

Without a word, I follow Glenn up the stairs. There's lead in my boots.

Everyone's waiting in Adam's room. The reporter looks like a sad old bastard who'd rather be anywhere else in the world. I know exactly how he feels.

He snaps some pictures of the four of us sitting on Adam's bed.

I refuse to smile and I'm still wearing my bathrobe over my clothes.

When the reporter leaves, the other guys are pissed off at me.

I don't care enough to even give it a second thought.

Fuck them.

PARTY WITH THE BEAUHUNKS

The Oshawa Times, Thursday, January 30, 1992

Last year, four young musicians got together to make some good music. The result is the Marvelous Beauhunks, one of the most promising new bands to emerge from the southern Ontario music scene.

Members Glenn Goodman, Stephen Closs, Stephen Wright, and Adam Graham spent their first year together writing material and playing selected shows in the Durham Region area. Since April 1991, the Marvelous Beauhunks have been performing numerous shows in cities across southern Ontario, including Peterborough, Oshawa, Ajax, Toronto, Burlington, and Hamilton.

In May, their song, Fantasy Merry-Go-Round, appeared on the 1991 CFNY Modern Music compilation release. The song reached number 16 on the weekly top 30 singles countdown.

The band has currently completed a six song cassette of original music, which was released this month on an independent label.

All the songs on the cassette were written and recorded between November 1990 and August 1991 at White Room Studios.

On Saturday, February 1, the Marvelous Beauhunks are having their cassette release party at Ultra Sound, 269 Queen Street West. CFNY is sponsoring the show.

The Marvelous Beauhunks self-titled cassette will be available at selected music stores in February.

MAJOR 'NY CHANGES

NOW Magazine, Thursday, January 30, 1992
T.O. Music Notes
Kim Hughes, James Marck, Tim Perlich

*In a surprise move, modern rock radio station **CFNY** general manager **Jamie Crookston** and program director **Reiner Schwarz** were fired last Tuesday morning—just one day prior to the release of industry barometer BBM Bureau of Measurement ratings, which showed CFNY with a devastatingly low market share.*

*According to the BBM report, CFNY's listenership nosedived to 3.4 percent in the fall of '91 from 4.8 in the spring of that year. Reports from CFNY insiders, who spoke on the promise of anonymity, said **Hal Blackadar**, president of KEY Radio, a division of MacLean Hunter, axed Crookston and Schwarz mid-morning Tuesday. Staff were advised not to comment to the press and repeated attempts to speak with Blackadar failed.*

Maybe new leadership can strike a balance between the station's weird mix of directionless programming—it's hard to be all things to all people—and its instances of overkill.

*After all, the **Barenaked Ladles** are great, but enough already.*

HUNK-MAIL NEWSLETTER (VOLUME 1, ISSUE 2)

Saturday, February 1, 1992

Hey folks!

It's time to roll another sheet of paper into the pawnshop typewriter and whip off another issue of Hunk Mail.

A lot has been happening at the red love shack in South Oshawa that the Marvelous Beauhunks call home. First off the cassette release party at UltraSound on Saturday, February 1. The show's presented by CFNY, and Brampton's The Coles are opening for the Beauhunks. The cassette will be available at the show for a measly $7.00 and should be in record stores the first week of February. Also available is the Marvelous Beauhunks line of casual wear, T-shirts for only $12.00.

The Marvelous Beauhunks have just wrapped up shooting their video for "Fantasy Merry-Go-Round." Producing and directing were a couple of real cool guys from Ryerson, Dave Kazala and Mike Wale. Release date is set for the end of February. Keep an eye out for the Beauhunks on the small screen.

The next month is gonna be a busy one for the Beauhunks. On the agenda is studio work, video work and a slew of shows. Upcoming performances include the Purple Onion in Oshawa on February 12, Heritage Theatre in Brampton with The Coles and Genetic Rhythm on February 22. If you want advance tickets for this one, talk to one of your friendly neighbourhood Beauhunks. On March 7, the Underdog in Peterborough is once again opening its doors to the Marvelous

Beauhunks. Word is that a few special interest groups in Peterborough are eagerly awaiting this night!

For helping us with the cassette and the live shows, there's a few people to thank. Like Sue, April, and John—merchandisers extraordinaire, Gorilla Phil for intros too numerous to mention, Hal, Joanne, and everyone at CFNY, fans and friends for continued support.

For more info on the Marvelous Beauhunks, write c/o 782unes, 782 Ritson Road South, Oshawa, Ontario L1H 5L1.

CFNY PRESENTS—MARVELOUS BEAUHUNKS CASSETTE RELEASE

UltraSound, Toronto—w/ the Coles
Saturday February 1, 1992

Tonight went off better than we could have hoped for. We successfully filled UltraSound on a Saturday night. It's a big accomplishment, and a huge relief. A lot of hard graft went into getting us here.

We played with confidence and control. Even Glenn laid off the booze until after the show. Our merchandising team was able to shift several cassettes and the last of our tee-shirts.

For the first time in a long time, I'm starting to feel a little bit better about the band. Tonight could possibly be a turning point. With an EP out and a video soon to follow, we're actually well positioned for a move to the next level—a recording contract with a major label.

The whole stigma of being one of the "five worst local acts" will soon be a memory.

I can breathe.

Monday (after work), February 3, 1992

Arriving home from work, I take my coat off as Adam walks out of his room. His face is stony.

"We're banned from UltraSound," he says.

"What?" I reply in disbelief. My ears are playing tricks on me.

"I said we're banned from ever playing UltraSound again. Not only are we banned from playing UltraSound, but we're also banned from the Horseshoe and X-Rays."

Adam explained that he'd called Yvonne earlier, to follow up after the show. He was expecting praise for Saturday's turnout. Instead of a warm invitation to book another gig, Yvonne's frosty tone was February personified.

"Ah no . . . we won't be having you back. You don't attract the right . . . . ah . . . *element*," she told him over the phone.

After our show, someone had ripped the sinks off the wall in the men's bathroom at X-Rays. The back door was kicked in, and pictures were smashed from the walls. The staff had been up all night mopping the water.

But she wasn't done yet.

Someone had smuggled alcohol into UltraSound. The bartenders complained that there were too many under-age punters in the club. Their liquor licence was at risk.

We're off Yvonne's "up-and-coming" list.

Forever.

But how is this our fault?

I want to throw up again.

BAND MEETING

Tuesday, February 4, 1992

Tonight's meeting is taking place upstairs, in the luxurious seven-eighty-two penthouse kitchen headquarters.

Aside from discussing our reputation-destroying ban from UltraSound, the main topic on the table is backing vocals for *Think It Over*. Should we bring Dave Parry into the studio this weekend to sing harmonies?

Steve says it'll make the song better. Adam thinks we should only have the actual band play on the recordings. Glenn doesn't care. I think both parties have good points and I'm still undecided.

I feel a kick under the table. Steve's looking directly into my eyes and nodding as he speaks.

"Steve Wright thinks Dave Parry should sing on it, don't you Steve?"

Adam's watching this exchange, fully aware of Steve's obvious attempt to deceive him. In Steve's defence, subtlety isn't exactly on his agenda tonight. He just wants to get his way.

The meeting comes to an end. Nothing's resolved.

In Adam's mind, Steve Closs is removed from the list of people he actually gives a shit about.

We're a happy family.

THINK IT OVER (Part 1)

Saturday, February 8, 1992

I'm so tired of Steve's prima donna attitude.

He's never on time. Today, we're all supposed to travel to the studio together. Damyana was scheduled to drop him off at seven-eighty-two over an hour ago.

Adam, Glenn and I are tired of waiting. Steve's an adult and he can get himself over to Scotty's. The three of us pile into my motor and leave for the studio.

When we arrive, we get busy setting up the gear and miking the drums. Thump-thump-thump. Scotty fiddles with the EQ's.

Adam sets his bass levels . . . . Dun-dun-dun-dun-dun.

The bass is ready to record.

Glenn's set up for his scratch vocal. Check . . . one-two . . . check. Sibilance. Bum-fun . . .

It's time for the guitars.

Steve's still not here.

Three hours have passed and there hasn't been a peep from him.

We complain about what a stubborn, passive-aggressive prick he is. Glenn phones Steve's house. Damyana calls Steve to the phone. He's angry that we didn't wait for him. Instead of coming to the studio, he went back home. Steve's not budging until one of us drives to his house and picks him up.

Even though it's costing us twenty-five dollars an hour to sit around waiting for him, I sure as hell won't go. Neither will Adam. Glenn's the first to blink and he asks to borrow my car.

Scotty shakes his head in the background.

When Glenn and Steve arrive, none of us are speaking to one another. We're already behind schedule so we get down to it. Someone still has to pick up Dave Parry.

By midnight, I've had enough of the studio and Adam and I go home. Glenn and Steve will catch a ride with Cathy on her way back from the Ozone.

All that's left to do is record the main vocal.

There's no way Steve and Glenn can possibly fuck that up.

THINK IT OVER (Part 2)

Sunday, February 9, 1992

This is horrible.

Laughable.

A catastrophe.

I can't believe my ears.

How in the world did you guys fuck this up?

After eight months of singing the main vocal one way, Glenn has recorded a new, improvised melody line for *Think It Over*.

Some of the words don't even make sense anymore.

All you guys had to do was sing the same fucking song the same fucking way as you've always done.

I give up.

No one wants to spend the time and money to have Glenn redo his vocal properly.

Fine.

If you guys don't see a problem with it, go ahead and mix it.

THE MARVELOUS BEAUHUNKS, Marvelous Beauhunks (782unes Music)

Oshawa/ Whitby This Week, Sunday Edition, February 9, 1992
By John Duarte

Oshawa's own and self-proclaimed, Marvelous Beauhunks have released a six song cassette on their own independent label. And, while this is a strong first effort, it is merely a promise of things to come.

. . .

Engineer Scott McClelland captures the feeling of this band by not overproducing the recording. He instead gives it a live-off-the-floor quality, which makes this type of music much more enjoyable.

. . .

Why am I not more excited about this?

What should be the beginning for us, is looking more like the end.

A promise of things to come . . . ?

More like *a promise of* what could've been.

Tuesday, February 11, 1992

I'm standing in the driveway of seven-eighty-two, smoking a cigarette and freezing my arse off. Adam's got the hood up on my Chevette. He's changing the oil filter. I watch without much interest.

Two girls from the Catholic high school are clocking us as they slowly walk by, clutching books to their chests. They whisper to each other, looking back, giggling.

I know exactly what's coming next.

"Are you guys in the Marvelous Beauhunks?" One of them asks shyly.

"FUCK OFF!" I bark, my lips pulled back in a hideous sneer.

Later Adam recounts the incident to Glenn with his usual shrill laughter.

"You can't do that!" Glenn admonishes me.

"Those are our fans!"

To me, that's part of the problem.

PURPLE ONION, OSHAWA—w/ One Word "Gottschliem"

Wednesday, February 12, 1992

Eleven months after our audition to open for the fake-Byrds, we're finally appearing at the world famous Purple Onion. The place is only a quarter full, and the manager's making us play straight through. Instead of two forty-five-minute sets like we normally do, we're playing a full one-hour-thirty-minute marathon. No stops, no breaks.

"Nobody plays two sets at the Purple Onion," commands the manager-man.

Against our better judgement, we go along with it. Lately we've become so tightly wound and desperate for success that every show is a make it or break it scenario. Instead of telling purple-onion-manager-man to lick our collective private parts, the once mighty Marvelous Beauhunks have rolled over on our backs, four paws to the air.

Steve's sullen and angry with me. Between each song, I chirp some bitter complaint into the microphone about playing this crap gig. My latest diatribe concerns my missing the NBC must-see Wednesday night line-up. He shoots me another dirty look as he tunes his guitar.

Glenn introduces *City Asleep*. Out of nowhere, a thick, white fog envelops Adam. I can hear the low-hiss of a smoke machine to the right of me. The smell of dry ice creeps into my nostrils. Adam's still playing his bass, but he's nowhere to be seen. Like the comely assistant in a cornball magic act, Adam has completely disappeared.

The fog drifts over my way and, soon, all I can see are coloured lights cutting through the mist. Halfway through the song, the smoke starts to dissipate. I can see Adam's outline. He's bent over double, heaving from laughing so hard. His mouth is wide open but no sound comes out. I'm forced to crack my first and last smile of the night.

Hello Cleveland.

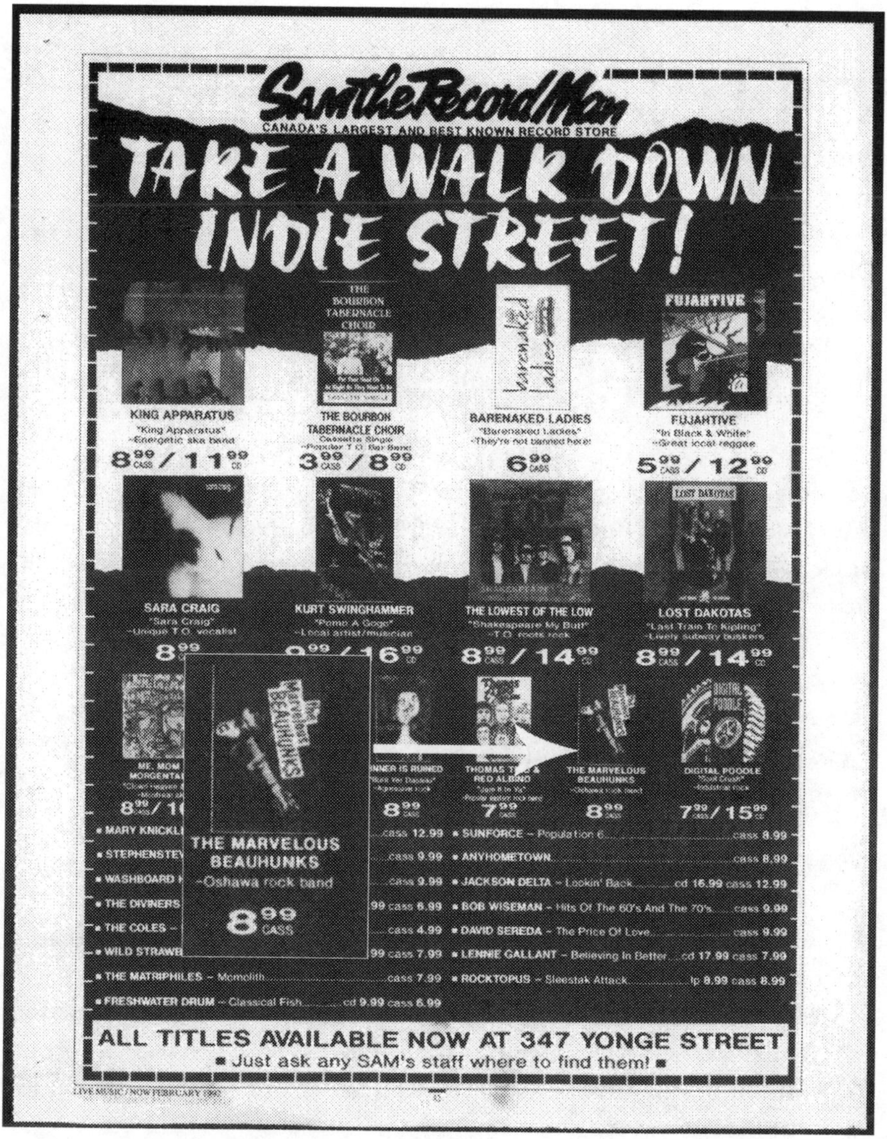

(Photo courtesy of NOW Magazine archives)

O'NEILL CVI, OSHAWA—VALENTINE'S DAY

Friday, February 14, 1992

OK. I'm a prostitute. Let's cut right to the chase and establish my price.

For the princely sum of $1,000, I've agreed to sell my soul and play the St. Valentine's Day dance at my former high school. Like Major Tom, I'm hitting an all-time low.

Before you get too excited about the fee, subtract $500 for the PA and sound man. Divide the remaining $500 by four. Now hand my portion back to Steve to hold for the costs of the *Fantasy Merry-Go-Round* video.

Why am I doing this? I'm almost 25 years old, and I'm performing for a bunch of teeny-boppers in the gymnasium of my old alma mater. Back in the day, Adam and Glenn also walked these hallowed halls. Steve went to a different high school.

Glenn's in his absolute glory. Me, I can hardly stand it for a minute longer. I couldn't stand it when we had to burst out of the ball-closet to take the stage in a gym full of screaming teenagers. I couldn't stand it when I saw the banner with our cartoon images on it, each of us wearing Roman garb, like togas or sandals. My image is kitted-out with a Caesar wreath and heart-adorned skivvies. It's a gruesome example of life imitating art since, right now, I'm actually wearing the same boxers as my cartoon counterpart.

Three numbers in, the kids are going insane like we're the Beatles at Shea Stadium. After each song, my old shop teacher threatens to shut the power down unless the crowd stops rushing the stage. As he gestures for them to back up, Adam and I notice that he's missing two fingers on one hand and another finger on the other. He's had an accident since Adam and I were in his class. So much for safety first. Now, the poor old bastard has to work crowd control at the Marvelous Beauhunks St. Valentine's Day Massacre.

We play a few more songs and the sound through the monitors suddenly becomes clearer. Scotty and Dave Parry have popped up at the sound board. They're three sheets to the wind, smiling and waving at us. Somehow, two drunken, strange, mid-30s men have blagged their way into a public high school and taken control of the PA by claiming to be our "producers." Security issues aside, it's good to see them.

At the end of our first set, we take a break. Adam and I stand outside in the smoking area and catch our breath. I do my best to project an air of inapproachability. It works. We rejoin Steve and Glenn in the boys locker room and get ready for round two.

When we retake the stage, we're assaulted with ear-splitting applause. Glenn steps up to the microphone for an announcement. Holding up a fist-full of industrial grade bathroom tissue, he proclaims to his loyal subjects:

"I can't believe you guys still have this kind of toilet paper here!"

Did he just say what I think he said?

His fans go wild.

What exactly did Glenn do during the break?

I know what it makes me think he did.

We've reached a new level of buffoonery. I've never felt worse about being in this band.

Glenn, on the other hand, thinks it was a great night.

He took the banner home with him.

Saturday, February 15, 1992

Back on the produce counter.

Yeah.

I'm a rock star.

Yeah.

I'm going to get a real job and do something with my life.

Yeah.

THINK IT OVER (dance club remix)

Sunday, February 16, 1992

No one wants to go to the studio.

Last weekend's mix of *Think It Over* was a failure. Nobody cares enough to go back and see it through. Steve's at the hospital with his dad and Adam's at Lisa's house. Glenn's hung-over again.

So it falls to me.

Think It Over is supposed to be this year's *Fantasy Merry-Go-Round*, our kick at the can for CFNY's 1992 Modern Music Search. Right now it's glossy, overproduced and it sounds like it's trying too hard. Maria's come with me to oversee this weekend's mix.

Scotty's tinkering at the console. He's got a creepy look on his face like Jack Nicholson in *the Shining*. *All work and no play . . .* It's unnerving. After five hours of studio trickery, *Think It Over* is still a turd. A well-polished turd, but a turd nonetheless.

Instead of following our instincts, we're trying to follow trends. There's talk of drum-loops, samples, and whether or not we need a deejay in the band.

We've officially lost the plot.

BREAK UP (PART 1)

Monday, February 17, 1992

As I get home from work, Adam's waiting for me by the door. This is getting to be a habit.

"You're not going to believe this," he says. "Glenn quit the band today."

I'm speechless.

That fucking rat bastard. For months I've been hanging on by the skin of my teeth. Any time I've mentioned quitting, I'm given the guilt trip.

You can't quit. The band will break up.

Now this selfish prick is packing it in?

"What did he say?" I seethe.

"He's going back to England to play football," Adam shrugs.

"Well if he's done, I'm done too." I say.

"If you're quitting, I'm quitting. There's no way I'm sticking it out with Closs," Adam declares.

"When do you want to tell him?"

"Tomorrow at practice." I wave Adam off.

I light a cigarette, switch on the TV and turn off my mind.

BREAK UP (PART 2)

Tuesday, February 18, 1992

"What do you mean you guys quit?"

Steve's shaking his head in disbelief. We're sitting at the kitchen table. He's still got his coat on.

"We just released a cassette and our video's almost done. We can't quit now."

He tries to persuade Adam and I to carry on without Glenn. I'm not having any of it.

"Then I'm going on without you guys. I'll find some new players to replace you."

That's Steve. Difficult to the end.

"That's fine," I say.

"We'll play the shows we've got booked, but that's it. I'm done."

Steve picks up his guitar case and goes home.

A chorus of angels are singing in my head. The weight of the world has been lifted from my weary shoulders. I put on my jacket and bid Adam a fond adieu. I head over to Maria's house, relieved that it's finally over.

What a waste of time.

THE RIVOLI, TORONTO (CANCELLED)—w/ Teknicolor Raincoats, Bugs Meany

Saturday, February 22, 1992

Steve's dad died so we're pulling out of this show. That leaves one last gig on the docket. The Underdog on Saturday, March 7th.

We've come full circle.

It seems appropriate to finish things there.

CFNY FM 102 PRESENTS CANADA'S BEST NEW MUSIC

Don Berns gave us a nice little eulogy on CFNY.

"So are the Marvelous Beauhunks the only group ever to come out of South Oshawa? Well they got together in February 1990, last year they made our modern music compilation with the song Fantasy Merry-Go-Round.

And this year, well they got in the studio and they started recording some new stuff and then I understand . . . they just broke up. Like the other day. They decided that's it, they're going to call it quits.

So this might be the last new music we hear from them, it's something they just recorded, called Dare to Dream. Canada's best new music today from Labatt's here's the Marvelous Beauhunks at CFNY."

Steve's pissed off that they played this. As far as he's concerned the band is still functioning because he's recruiting new players.

I suppose he figures nobody's going to notice.

BEAUHUNKS ARE BACK

The Wire, Vol. 3, No. 5, February 28 to March 13, 1992.

*Those irrepressible good time guys from Oshawa, the **Marvelous Beauhunks**, are making another trip up the 115 on Saturday to play the Underdog.*

*The **Beauhunks,** who marry contemporary music with vintage guitar, appeared on the 1991 Modern Music compilation with their single Fantasy Merry-Go-Round. Last month, they released their first independent cassette on the 782unes music label, available for sale in Toronto, Oshawa, and Peterborough music outlets.*

This month will also mark the Beauhunks' video debut with the release of their video for Fantasy Merry-Go-Round.

UPPER SEVEN-EIGHTY-TWO

Thursday, March 5, 1992

Adam and I had a great idea.

On two of our Marvelous Beauhunks shirts, we've painted black bars across the eyes of everyone on the tee-shirt except for Steve.

On the back of the shirts are the tour dates for the "Kramer vs. Kramer Tour." There's just one date: Saturday, March 7th, 1992, in "Anama City" or "Animosity" for the phonetically gifted.

We'll keep them under our regular shirts until the last song.

Fuck Steve for thinking he can just replace us all and keep calling it the Marvelous Beauhunks.

THE KRAMER VS. KRAMER TOUR (PART 1)

Saturday, March 7, 1992

"Hey, when's your video coming out?" asks the excited punter.

"I don't know. You'll have to ask Steve Closs. He's the leader of this band," says Adam.

This is our standard answer to every question. It doesn't matter if Steve is standing in front of us or not. Tonight, will not go down easily.

On the other hand, Glenn's acting as though this is just another day in the magical, fairytale land of the Marvelous Beauhunks. As usual, he doesn't have a care in the world. I've long given up trying to figure him out.

Adam and I are biding our time until we're officially ex-MBH, a distinction I'm looking forward to.

"I don't know. Ask Steve Closs. He's the leader of this band."

The Underdog is packed to capacity. Everything is going surprisingly smoothly. Glenn's enjoying himself to the point that I'm wondering if he's reconsidered his resignation and intends to carry on with Steve. But all I truly care about is getting through the last song. To be free of this life.

At long last, the time is right. Adam and I are ready to throw the gates of hell wide open. We casually remove our long sleeve shirts to reveal the black-barred "Kramer vs. Kramer" shirts we so carefully constructed.

Steve, this is our loving tribute to you.

We watch him for his reaction. Steve soaks it in, expressionless. He ignores us and tunes his guitar. I'm disappointed.

Steve steps up to the microphone to introduce the last song.

"Tonight is the last performance of the Marvelous Beauhunks with this line-up."

Groans and boos come from the crowd.

"Some of the members of this band are leaving to pursue successful careers as vegetable washers."

His comment is meant to inflict maximum pain and he's successful. I fly into a rage. With no regard for how we look, I start playing *Pictures and Tears* at supersonic speed. Steve locks eyes with me and he's not backing down. This is the moment of ugly finality. An uncomfortable showdown is playing out in full view of the audience. The punters don't realize they're witnessing the dissolution of a band, a friendship and a dream. They wait to see what happens next.

Like a wraith, Adam steps out of the red light that's consumed my vision. He starts to drag the tempo down, nodding at me to join him. Let's finish this thing right.

My pulse starts to slow and my chest begins to loosen. I feel like I'm coming out from under a tidal wave. My breathing is regular again. The world switches from slow motion into real time.

Adam and I lock in and find our groove.

We finish the song.

Beauhunk-style.

THE KRAMER VS. KRAMER TOUR (revisited)

Saturday, March 7, 1992

"You guys are fucking cunts—I mean it!"

Holy shit.

Adam and I look at each other with eyebrows raised, our jaws gaping. We're stunned. In the whole time we've known him, Glenn has never spoken to anyone like that. Certainly not to us.

Moments ago, we finished playing our last song ever as a band and I'm vaguely aware of the applause that's coming from the crowd. Glenn's face is twisted into a vicious-looking snarl and I'm dumbfounded. Is he for fucking real?

As of right now, I hate Steve Closs with every fiber of my being. We barely made it through the last number without punching the crap out of each other and, now, Glenn wants to play "mod-god" and do an encore. The last thing I want is to put on a happy face and be the nice little drummer-boy for someone else's ego trip.

I just want to get the fuck out of here. Fast.

So when Adam and I refused to keep playing, Glenn called us cunts. I'd laugh out loud if I weren't so shocked.

In the background, the punters are chanting "Wipe Out . . . ! Wipe Out . . . ! Wipe Out . . . !" and they're going mad. After all this, they wanted an encore. Well, the punters can all go fuck themselves as far as I'm concerned.

I look at Adam and shrug my shoulders in resignation. I begin to knock out the intro to *Like Wow—Wipe Out*, by the Hoodoo Gurus, and a howl of satisfaction reverberates throughout the club. Without an ounce of effort on his part, Glenn casually transformed back into his persona of good-natured geezer and set about singing his encore.

Absolutely fucking surreal.

The Underdog has no stage so there's nothing to separate us from the beer-soaked lunatics hanging from the rafters. Those in the crowd who can still stand are pressed shoulder to shoulder, and they're dancing maniacally as Adam, Steve and I begrudgingly deliver them their stupid fucking song. Glenn smiles, sings and slaps hands with the crowd.

This time when the song is over and before anyone else can say a word to stop me, I tear down my kit and load my drums out the side-door and into the back of my car as fast as I can. I don't say goodbye to anyone and no one says goodbye to me. Fucking assholes.

It takes nearly an hour to drive home. My girlfriend Maria and I sit in the dark and ride along in silence. She tries to say some comforting things to me, but I'm really not in the mood to hear anything positive. My emotion-meter is buried in the red, charged with an alternating current of anger, humiliation and relief. I don't know which one is the most prevalent. They're all taking turns beating me up. Except for relief. Relief is actually taking it pretty easy on me.

For the first time in over two years, I've humped my drums up the stairs and into an empty corner of my flat instead of the band's rehearsal space down in the basement. I throw off my sweat-soaked T-shirt and put on a cup of tea. How the hell had things gotten so fucked up? It wasn't supposed to happen this way.

I wash the cup, crush out my cigarette and go to bed. I fall asleep a rock 'n' roll star but, when I wake up in the morning, I'm just another sad-sack, under-employed nobody.

Welcome to the working week.

Tuesday, March 9, 1992

Mike and Dave, the video producers, have been calling. The video for *Fantasy Merry-Go-Round* is complete and they're looking for payment.

Adam told them that the band broke up and we don't need it anymore. That didn't go over too well. He tells them that we're going to sell off our PA and they'll have to wait until then to collect their money.

They're pissed-off.

Rightfully so, but I've got bigger things to worry about. Like finding a job.

God knows, I can't wash vegetables for the rest of my life.

Thursday, March 11, 1992

Steve wants the PA.

We tell him, through Glenn, that he can have it. So long as he takes over the debt for the video.

Steve agrees and I make sure to stay upstairs the day he picks it up from the basement.

The video and the Marvelous Beauhunks are Steve's problem to deal with from now on.

Asshole.

PART 3
THE AFTERMATH

NATIONAL CHART FOR THE COLLEGE/ ALTERNATIVE/ INDEPENDENT MUSIC TRADE

March 1992, Volume 2, Issue 10

THE MARVELOUS BEAUHUNKS—self-titled (782unes music)-Jim Shorkey

"Fantasy Merry-Go-Round" is a throbbing musical workout that would sound great on a sweaty rave or on an open highway. That's a pretty big sound from four boys from Oshawa. And that song is not a fluke. This six-song release has a sense of promise that is just starting to be realized. The songs are strong and hook laden. The performance is lively and just loose enough to hint that these guys must really cook live. The combo of singer Glenn Goodman's honeyed voice and Stephen Closs' Rickenbackers creates a familiar but distinct sound. The musicianship is very good but what really makes the recording standout is its sense of fun.

CJIV 93.9 FM—SIMON FRASER UNIVERSITY, Burnaby B.C.

March 17, 1992

Hi,

Read about your release in National Chart and thought I'd request an airplay copy.

Sounds like fun.

Thanks,

John Clark
Music Coordinator.

MODERN MUSIC SHOWDOWN

EYE Weekly, April 16, 1992

NY's ***Modern Music Search*** *1992 is a step closer to completion with playback of the top 50 semi-finalists beginning Monday (April 20). Selected from a staggering 450 entries, the finalists include* ***Genetic Rhythm, 49 Acres, The Waltons, 98 DA, Morbidox, Saturnalia, One, Flatland, Monkey Trial, Sour Landslide, All Good Children, Teknicolor Raincoats, Bourbon Tabernacle Choir, Fujahtive, Anyhowtown, hHead, Scam Artists, Waiting for Jane, Marvelous Beauhunks, FunkINC, The Coles, Ten Commandments****, and* ***Sheltering Sky.***

Ten finalists will be announced May 18 and they'll play at the CD release party and showcase slated for June 4 at the Phoenix.

WEDGE OF THE WEEK

April 1992

The *Fantasy Merry-Go-Round* video is "Wedge of the Week" on MuchMusic.

RECONCILIATION

May 1992

I've come to the conclusion that I don't really want my friendship with Steve to be over. If anyone's going to open a dialogue, it'll have to be me. It's not Steve's style and, after the *Kramer vs. Kramer Tour*, who can blame him.

Sucking up my pride, I drive to his house. I climb the back stairs and knock on the door. Steve opens it.

"I'm glad that you came by," he says. "Because I wasn't going to."

"I know you weren't," I reply.

We shake hands.

We're friends again.

MARVELOUS FAUXHUNKS

Saturday, May 23, 1992

Through our old vocal teacher, Dave Parry, Steve's recruited two new band members; Steve Steele on bass, and Jeremy Summers on drums. Both are excellent players.

The new Beauhunks are a more musically proficient unit than the original cast . . . a three-piece band, with Steve doing a competent job on lead vocal. Steve, it turns out, is a much better singer than Glenn. Even so, he still doesn't have Glenn's charisma. Glenn's the superior frontman.

On Saturday, Glenn, Adam and I went to see them play at Sneaky Dee's, with Box Meat Revolution. Although we were there mostly to support Steve, we still wanted to take the piss out of him. Anticipating this, Damyana planted herself at our table, making it impossible for us to take any shots at him.

The new MBH did a good show, but it was weird to watch it from our perspective. It was strangers playing our songs—the songs the four of us had worked so hard to create. They may have been performed well, but it wasn't the real deal. It was cabaret.

The "No-Hunks" appeared once more on Breakfast Television, playing *Think It Over* and *Coffee-Maker*. Watching them on TV solidified for me that the magic and the chemistry were gone. I was well and truly glad to be finished with it.

When *Think It Over* failed to make 1992's CFNY Modern Music disc, Steve put paid to the Marvelous Beauhunks for good. Before they'd even play their last gig, Steve would already be in the process of forming Dionysian Smile, with the singer from Genetic Rhythm.

Steve offered me a spot in the new group, but my heart wasn't in it. My path lay in a different direction. I'd write my own songs and record them by myself, with me playing all the instruments. That way, I'd never be at the mercy of someone else's fucked up personality again.

Lightning would strike twice, I told myself.

After all, I was the true talent behind the Marvelous Beauhunks.

CFNY SHAKE-UP

NOW Magazine, Thursday, June 25, 1992
T.O. Music Notes
Kim Hughes, James Marck, Tim Perlich

Regular ***CFNY*** *listeners have undoubtedly noticed some high-profile voices—morning man* ***Skot Turner****, afternoon drive guy* ***Don Berns****, Live in Toronto host* ***Kneale Mann*** *and news director* ***Rick Charles*** *haven't been beaming in from the Brampton station this week.*

That's because, as of Tuesday, eight 'NY staffers had, in the words of VP and general manager ***Vince DiMaggio****, "their working relationships terminated on a one-to-one basis for individual reasons," all of which must have been pretty major. Turner has been at the station for eight years; Mann for seven and Charles for roughly twelve. Currently, general staff is filling in the gaps.*

DiMaggio denied that the spring BBM ratings—released in June and showing CFNY up in its overall ratings from last fall but down from last spring—had anything to do with the firings. "The motivation for this," says DiMaggio, "is based on reorganization and restructuring. These are tough decisions reflecting tough economic times."

Not surprisingly, that doesn't jibe with the buzz on the street. A source at the station, who asked not to be named, suggests the firings were more a reflection of strained internal relationships among those fired and the station brass. When contacted, Turner outlined his impressive involvement with the station, noting he is, "the only full-time announcer at CFNY ever to achieve the number one position in the Toronto market." Turner added, he's now on board at ***Dance 108*** *as assistant program director. Other ex-employees contacted by NOW would not go on the record.*

DiMaggio is non-committal on the issue of potential format changes, saying, "Nothing in the future indicates format changes, but we'll have to wait and see. When different people go there are always changes." CFNY has been cleaning house all year—the new year found program director **Reiner Schwarz** *and general manager* **Jamie Crookston** *canned unexpectedly, along with other key staffers, when poor fall ratings rolled in.*

On another note, CFNY director of Canadian talent development **Hal Harbour** *resigned June 11 for what DiMaggio describes as "personal reasons." But there was no bad blood, he was* **not** *fired, and we intend to work with each other again in the future."*

With so many profile players out of the picture, it'll be interesting to see what CFNY's next move will be—and how many people will be tuned in to hear it.

SOCAN

Friday, August 14, 1992

Finally received my first royalty cheque from SOCAN today.

Twelve-dollars and sixty-two cents.

I'm riding on a *Fantasy Merry-Go-Round.*

Too fucking funny.

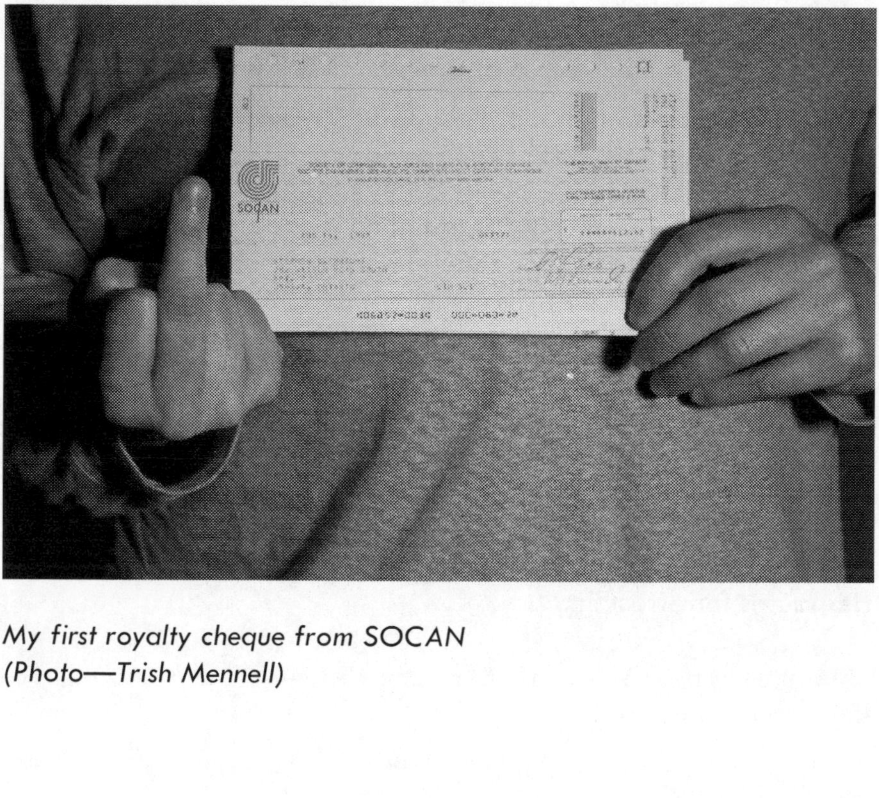

My first royalty cheque from SOCAN
(Photo—Trish Mennell)

SUMMER IN THE CITY

August 1992

Adam bursts through the door of seven-eighty-two and leaps up the stairs, taking them two at a time.

"You'll never guess what happened today. Hahaha!" He cackles.

It's a scalding afternoon in August and I'm too miserable to be playing silly guessing games. He ignores my disinterested grunt and continues on with his story.

"I was at the Oshawa Centre. I went into Sam the Record Man to look at CD's, and there was these two teenage girls looking at our tape," he continues.

"I overhear one girl say to the other girl, 'Didn't the Marvelous Beauhunks just break up?'"

He pauses for effect . . .

"The other girl says, 'Yeah. I hear one of them's got AIDS'. I nearly shit myself. Hahahahaha."

Do not resuscitate.

PART 4
FAINT HEARTBEATS, NO BRAINWAVES

STILL THINKING IT OVER

April 1995

It still bothers me that *Think It Over* was left in such a sorry state when we broke up.

Today, it's time to remedy that. The bed tracks are solid and the backing vocals are tight. There's tambourine, maracas and 12-string Rickenbacker all over the place. All the song really needs is a tougher main guitar line and a lead vocal that's not butchered by last-minute melody changes and mispronounced lyrics.

I call Scotty and foot the bill for some studio time. Steve, Glenn and Adam all participate, eager to make *Think It Over* into the song that it should've been in the first place.

On Saturday, things go according to plan. Steve lays down his new guitar line and adds a few new interesting twists. Since Adam's bass parts were done right the first time, he hangs out with Scotty behind the mixing desk.

To prepare Glenn for his vocals, I take him outside to my car. We listen to old cassettes of us playing the song live.

"Just do it like that and it'll sound awesome," I tell him.

"Yeah," he agrees.

We wrap for the day. We plan to start again at noon tomorrow, and Glenn will record his vocal.

He never shows up.

Steve does the main vocal instead.

Although I'm pissed-off at Glenn, the song actually sounds better with Steve singing it.

WORK (BUT NOT THE SUPERMARKET)

July 1996

We've got a summer student at work. He's seven or eight years younger than me. I'm old enough to be his supervisor, but still young enough to talk music with. It turns out that we like a lot of the same groups. In passing, I mention that I used to play the clubs back in the day.

"What was your band?" He asks.

"Ah, you wouldn't have heard of us," I reply, not wanting to pursue it.

Truth be told, I'm a little embarrassed by my past as a "band guy" . . . especially in a band called "the Marvelous Beauhunks." I own a house with my girlfriend and I'm trying to build a career. The last thing I need is to be outed as an ex-Beauhunk. It doesn't seem dignified.

So I tell him.

"What!? I love you guys!"

My cover is blown.

"I'm on the homecoming committee at Western and we're getting a big band like 'Spirit of the West' to play in the fall. Would you guys consider getting back together to open for them?" He asks excitedly.

As further incentive he adds, “You’d be playing in front of, like, two thousand people.”

Even with all the bad memories floating around my frontal lobes, I find myself getting the itch. Maybe enough time has gone by. Maybe we could finally make this work.

My first call is to Steve. He’s left Dionysian Smile. His musical plate is empty.

“Yeah. I’ll do it.”

One down, two to go.

I phone Gooders. I know his response before I even ask the question. He’s been waiting for this call for the past four years.

“I’m in.”

Two down.

Adam will be the wildcard. I know he was done with the band the first time around. There’s no love lost between him and Steve. But he surprises me.

“Aw, fuck! I guess so.”

Maybe, he just wants something new to complain about.

Just like that, we’re back.

I tell the kid at work to count us in for homecoming.

I make some initial inquiries about rehearsal space and drum rentals. I don’t even have my old P.O.S. Tama’s anymore. Before I can book a single practice, the phone starts ringing.

Steve has a list of conditions and demands. Then Glenn phones me with his list. The phone rings again. It's Adam with his own "I don't want to play if . . ." list.

I tell the summer student from Western that we're out. I go back to work.

It should have been so easy, but of course it isn't. We don't want to win. We like it better when we lose.

It's more comfortable that way.

PART
5
—RESUSCITATION—
2010

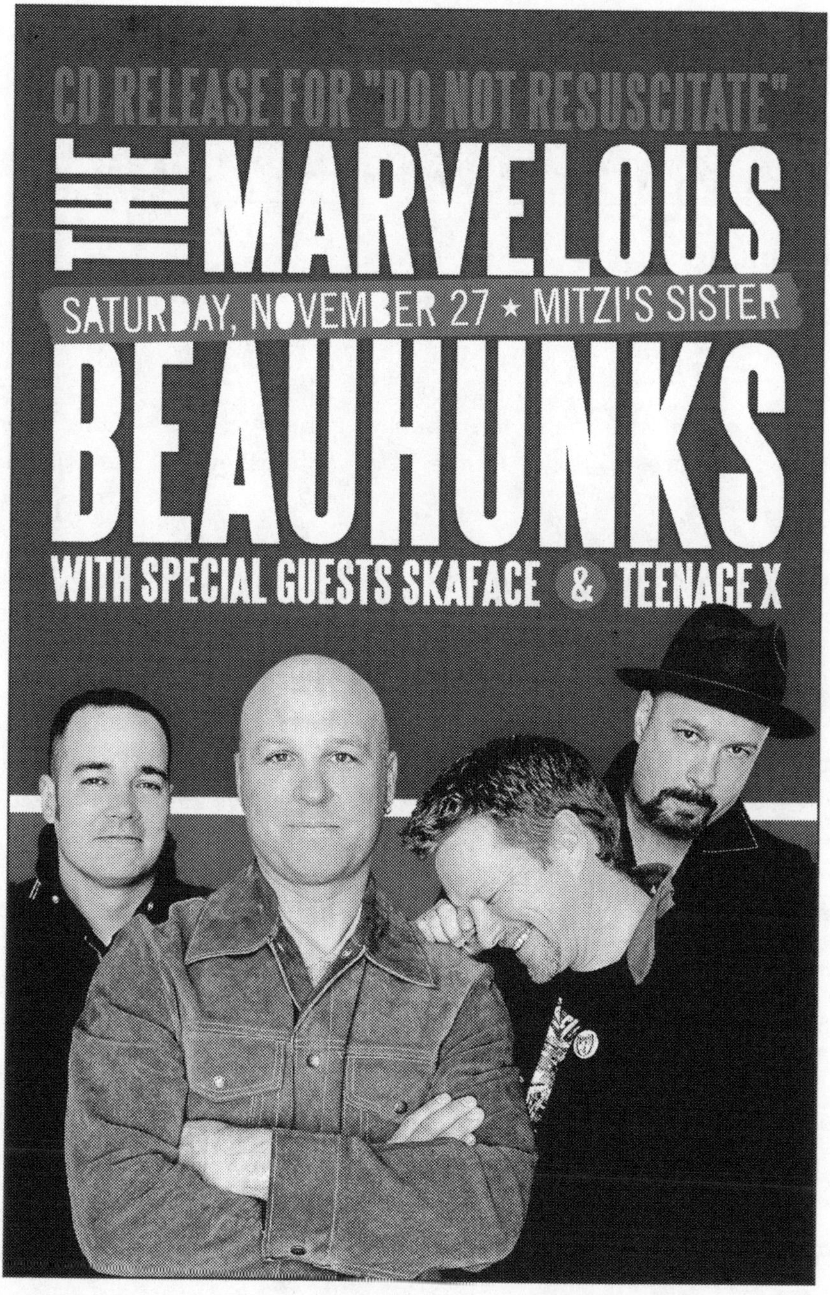

(Phil Butler—poster design, Trish Mennell—photo)

MITZI'S SISTER, TORONTO—w/ SKAFACE, Teenage X

Saturday, November 27, 2010

Steve is gently strumming the opening chords to *Pictures and Tears*. None of us are oblivious to the irony of starting the set with this particular song.

Derek steps up to the microphone.

"Fuck! I didn't think I'd ever be doing this job again.

Nineteen ninety-one was a wild year for us, for the Beauhunks. There was love, hate, sex, drugs, controversy. Highs, lows and the end of an era. The band split and everyone pretty much hated everyone.

Now, 20 years have gone by. Time has stood still for no man. But tonight, for one night only, they are here for you—breaking 18 years of silence.

Ladies and gentlemen . . . THE MARVELOUS BEAUHUNKS!!"

I count us in 1,2,3,4 . . . and the music starts again.

Give me 400 kilojoules. Clear!

Again.

Clear!

Increase to 500.

We've got a pulse.

BP is one-twenty over eighty.

Heartbeat is strong.

We're back, motherfuckers.

We're back.

Marvelous Beauhunks in 2010—Stephen Wright, Stephen Closs, Glenn Goodman, Fab Claxton
(Photo—Trish Mennell)

EPILOGUE

At the time of writing this cautionary tale, I'm 44 years old. It seems like a lifetime ago that the events of this book took place. Given that I was only 22 when Steve and I formed the group with Adam and Glenn, I suppose it really has been a lifetime.

Where have all the good times gone?

I'd like to point out that what I've written here serves only to recount my memories of how things went down with the MBH. Dates, people and places have been exhaustively researched for accuracy. In the event that a particular date was impossible to find, my best estimate was substituted. For the time being, my version of events is the only written account of what it was like to be in the Marvelous Beauhunks. The other guys might have something else to say. Feel free to ask them.

Given the once-in-a-lifetime opportunity that five dumb kids from Oshawa were handed, it may be hard for outsiders to feel any sympathy for us. We were offered our dreams on a platter and we acted like brats. We pissed all over each other and then wondered why things didn't work out. But given who we were, it truly couldn't have turned out any other way.

Today, I'm proud of what we achieved with the Marvelous Beauhunks. Though, if I could do it all again, I'd change how I dealt with my small brush with fame. Arrogance in a young man can be cool, but humility is far cooler. Medication helps.

Looking back from a distance of over two decades, it's clear to see how we all played our roles in the successes of the band, and how we all played our parts in it's messy demise. It's equal shares all around.

And that's the way it should be.

Finally, in case you're wondering—I don't work in supermarkets anymore.

SCW

Author, Stephen Wright—2011
(Photo—Trish Mennell)

The Marvelous Beauhunks are:

1990-1992

Glenn Goodman—vocals
Stephen Closs—guitar
Adam Graham—bass
Stephen Wright—drums

Derek Supryka—management

2010-Present

Glenn Goodman—vocals, guitar
Stephen Closs—guitar
Fab Claxton—bass
Stephen Wright—drums

Derek Supryka—management

(Photo—Trish Mennell)

WHAT EVER HAPPENED TO . . .?

Stephen Closs—Played guitar for Dionysian Smile and Leviride. Holds a senior, global position in the pharmaceutical industry. Lives in Durham Region with his wife and four boys. Hockey dad and guitar-player for the MBH.

Glenn Goodman—Went on to sing in the Jack Trippers and the Mod Stewarts. Owns and operates an agricultural business in rural Ontario, where he lives with his wife and two kids. Marvelous Beauhunks' frontman.

Adam Graham—Married Lisa in 1994. Currently works in the nuclear power industry and lives in the Greater Toronto Area with Lisa and their daughter. Adam hasn't picked up a bass since March 7, 1992 and that's how he likes it.

Derek Supryka—Has lived/worked in France, Japan, Australia, the United States, Scotland and England. Derek has held the following positions: record label executive, art director, photographer, kindergarten teacher, superstar travelling DJ, coach, music producer, graphic designer, real estate tycoon, thug, drummer, managing director, journalist, archivist, historian, project manager, and dad. Once and present manager for the Marvelous Beauhunks.

Stephen Wright—E.learning developer and graphic designer. Dad. Lives in Toronto. Keeps the beat that shuffles your feet. Drummer for the Marvelous Beauhunks.

The Coles—Rich currently plays in the great Teenage X. Vince went on to form the critically acclaimed Sour Landslide during the '90s and is now singing in the Benvereens. Drummer Sean is an award-winning filmmaker. Some of his work includes videos for Billy Talent and Good Charlotte. Not sure what Darren's up to.

SKAFACE—Still skanking. One of the coolest bands I've had the privilege of sharing a stage with.

hHead—Were signed by IRS Records in 1994. Broke up in 1997. One of the guys formed Broken Social Scene.

Monday Nuns—Became the Killjoys in 1992. Had hits with the singles *Today I Hate Everyone*, and *Dana*. Won a Juno Award for "Best New Group" in 1997.

Sloan—Twelve records out so far. When they released the excellent *Twice Removed*, Steve Closs was convinced that they'd stolen their sound from us. If you see Steve on a barstool today, don't get him started if you know what's good for you.

Barenaked Ladies—We all know what happened to them.

Jeremy Summers—is the Chief Marketing Officer and Executive VP of Interscope Geffen A&M in Los Angeles, working on marketing campaigns for artists such as Lady Gaga. Go figure.

RECORDINGS

CFNY Modern Music 1991
CFNY CDNT—C506
CD and Cassette
1991

Track Listing:

1. I.C.E.—*Strange Attractor*
2. The Marvelous Beauhunks—*Fantasy Merry-Go-Round*
3. SKAFACE—*Sometimes*
4. The Coles—*Crashing Down*
5. Pray for Rain—*Pocketful of Dreams*
6. Digital Poodle—*Work Terminal*
7. The Cynix—*Winds of Courage*
8. Ben McPeek—*A Walk Along The Boardwalk*
9. Sing Along With Tonto—*6+6+7*
10. Saturnalia—*Wait By The Water*
11. The Fringe—*Lookin' For More*
12. Chris Bottomley—*Seize The Day*
13. Smalltown Preachers—*Claudine Had A Freaky Hat*
14. Digit—*Guardian*
15. Suffer Machine—*Heartwar*

The Marvelous Beauhunks—S/T

782unes Music—MBH-001
Cassette
1992

Track Listing:

1. *Fantasy Merry-Go-Round*
2. *Dare to Dream*
3. *City Asleep*
4. *Pictures and Tears*
5. *Kickin' Around*
6. *TYNL*

The Marvelous Beauhunks—Do Not Resuscitate

782unes Music—MFA21819
CD and digital download (iTunes, CD Baby, Bandcamp, Amazon)
2010

Track Listing:

1. *Fantasy Merry-Go-Round*
2. *Pictures and Tears*
3. *Dare to Dream*
4. *Think It Over*
5. *Kickin' Around*
6. *City Asleep*
7. *TYNL*
8. *Undercover Girl*
9. *Holly (I'm not your friend)*
10. *Fantasy Merry-Go-Round* (Live)
11. *Pictures and Tears* (Live)
12. *TYNL* (Live)
13. *Outro*

(Photo—Trish Mennell)

THE SONGS

Set List—Originals

TYNL
Dare to Dream
City Asleep
Pictures and Tears
Fantasy Merry-Go-Round
Kickin' Around
Think It Over
What's All This Noise About Nothing?
Coming Down
Remains to be Scene
Same Old Story
Coffee-Maker

Set List—Covers

I'm Cryin'—the Animals
We Gotta Get Out of This Place—the Animals
Heart Full of Soul—Yardbirds
My Mind Goes Round in Circles—Squire
Debbie Jones—Squire
Ready Steady Go—Generation X
Happy Together—the Jam
Life From a Window—the Jam
Pressure Drop—the Clash
My Biggest Thrill—Mighty Lemon Drops
A Wish Away—Wonderstuff
Give Me More—Wonderstuff

Like Wow Wipe Out—Hoodoo Gurus
Two Swords—English Beat
Click Click—English Beat
Nice Legs (Shame About Her Face)—the Monks
Blues From a Gun—Jesus and Mary Chain
Little Bitch—the Specials
What'd I Say?—Ray Charles
Gloria—Them
Money—the Beatles
Pretty Vacant—Sex Pistols
Run, Run, Run—the Who

MARVELOUS BEAUHUNKS 1.0—LIVE DATES

Cameron House, Toronto (Cancelled)—w/ Map of Dreams
Monday, June 4, 1990

Pizza Pino's, Ajax—w/ MIU
Saturday, August 18, 1990

Closs/Metez Wedding
Saturday, August 25, 1990

Pizza Pino's, Ajax—w/ the Mindset
Saturday, December 22, 1990

Underdog, Peterborough—w/ the Mindset
Saturday, February 2, 1991

Stratengers, Toronto—w/ the Life
Sunday, April 7, 1991

El Mocambo, Toronto—w/ Lost Tribe, the Fact
Tuesday, April 9, 1991

Marquee, Toronto—w/ the Mindset, Heebee Gee
Tuesday, April 16, 1991

Trent Music Festival, Peterborough—w/ 28 bands
Friday, April 26, 1991

Stratengers, Toronto—w/ the Life
Wednesday, May 15, 1991

Sound of Music Festival, Burlington—w/ Monday Nuns

Thursday, May 30, 1991

Pig's Ear, Burlington—w/ the Corndogs
Friday, May 31, 1991

East Shore Community Centre, Pickering—w/ hHead, the Mindset, Heebee Gee
Sunday, June 9, 1991

Stratengers, Toronto—w/ Smalltown Preachers
Thursday, July 4, 1991

Marquee, Toronto—w/ the Monday Nuns
Thursday, July 11, 1991

Lee's Palace, Toronto—w/ the Life, Surrender Dorothy
Saturday, July 20, 1991

Corktown Tavern, Hamilton—w/ Monday Nuns, Cockleshell Heroes
Wednesday, July 25, 1991

UltraSound, Toronto—w/ Trouble With Jan
Monday, July 29, 1991

Silver Dollar, Toronto—w/ Scam Artists, Heebee Gee
Friday, August 2, 1991

UltraSound, Toronto—w/ the Coles, Smalltown Preachers (CFNY Live Recording)
Thursday, August 22, 1991

Niagara House, Toronto—w/ the Coles, Portable Ethnic Taxi
Friday, August 30, 1991

Marquee, Toronto—w/ Scam Artists, Voodoo Chicken
Saturday, August 31, 1991

Lee's Palace, Toronto—w/ Transvision Vamp (UK)

Wednesday, September 4, 1991

Apocalypse Club, Toronto—w/ SKAFACE, Cadillac Bill & the Creeping Bent
Friday, September 13, 1991

Underdog, Peterborough—w/ Voodoo Chicken (Hide Your Daughters Tour)
Saturday, September 21, 1991

Stratengers, Toronto—w/ Pasty White Boys
Thursday, September 26, 1991

Underdog, Peterborough—w/ All Good Children (Alan Alda Sensitive Guy Tour)
Friday, November 1, 1991

Star Club, Oshawa—w/ the Cynics (Pittsburgh, PA)
Saturday, November 9, 1991

Sneaky Dee's, Toronto—w/ Snowdogs, The Coles, Sarcastic Mannequins
Friday, November 15, 1991

Clinton's, Toronto—w/ SKAFACE
Friday, November 29, 1991

Silver Dollar—w/ Genetic Rhythm
Friday, December 6, 1991

Phoenix Concert Theatre, Toronto—w/ SKAFACE, the Coles, ICE (CFNY Presents the Bramchester Beat Xmas Party)
Wednesday, December 18, 1991

Pizza Pino's, Ajax—w/ the Mindset
Saturday, December 21, 1991

Lee's Palace, Toronto—w/ SKAFACE, the Coles
Friday, January 3, 1991

Clinton's, Toronto—w/ Genetic Rhythm (video release for *Time is Perverse*)
Thursday, January 9, 1992

Breakfast Television (*Citytv*), Toronto—performed *Fantasy Merry-Go-Round, Pictures and Tears*
Tuesday, January 28, 1992

UltraSound, Toronto—w/ the Coles (CFNY Presents Cassette Release)
Saturday, February 1, 1992

Purple Onion, Oshawa—w/ One Word "Gottschliem"
Wednesday, February 12, 1992

O'Neill Collegiate and Vocational Institute, Oshawa
Friday, February 14, 1992

Rivoli, Toronto (Cancelled)—w/ Teknicolor Raincoats, Bugs Meany
Saturday, February 22, 1992

Underdog, Peterborough—w/ Genetic Rhythm (Kramer vs. Kramer Tour)
Saturday, March 7, 1992

MARVELOUS BEAUHUNKS 2.0—LIVE DATES

Ozone, Oshawa
Date unknown, 1992

Sneaky Dee's, Toronto—w/ Fish Pants
Monday, May 18, 1992

Sneaky Dee's, Toronto—w/ Box Meat Revolution
Saturday, May 23, 1992

Breakfast Television (*Citytv*)—performed *Think It Over, Coffee-Maker*
Tuesday, May 26, 1992

El Mocambo, Toronto—w/ Genetic Rhythm, Scam Artists
Thursday, May 28, 1992

Opera House, Toronto—CFNY presents—w/ Genetic Rhythm, Pariahs
Sunday, June 20, 1992

MARVELOUS BEAUHUNKS 3.0—LIVE DATES

Mitzi's Sister, Toronto—w/ SKAFACE, Teenage X
Saturday, November 27, 2010

Horseshoe Tavern, Toronto—w/ the Cunningham's, Crimes in Paris, Funksway
Tuesday, February 22, 2011

Mitzi's Sister, Toronto—w/ the Targets (UK), the 905s
Friday, March 25, 2011

Murphy's Pub and Grill, Oshawa—w/ Crummy Stuff, Ultimatemost High, Viva Mars
Saturday, March 26, 2011

DO NOT RESUSCITATE – Book Release Party
Robert McLaughlin Gallery, Oshawa—w/ Viva Mars
Friday, May 4, 2012

WEB

www.782unes.com

www.wardourmedia.com

ACKNOWLEDGEMENTS

Many people contributed to the making of this book either with their time, encouragement, or both.

To Hal Harbour and Joanne Faloona from CFNY. Without you guys, there wouldn't be much of a story to tell. Thanks for taking a chance on us. Sorry we let you down.

John Duarte, who wrote the first feature article about the Marvelous Beauhunks, and many others throughout 1991-92. Excellent editing job on the book, John. I'm much obliged.

Marvelous Beauhunks manager, extraordinaire, Derek Supryka. Thanks for being so forthcoming with your memories, suggestions, reads and rereads. Your ability to think around a problem helped me get this project out the door.

My friends and bandmates . . . Stephen Closs, Adam Graham and Glenn Goodman. What can I say? It wasn't always fun, but it was never dull. I'm proud of what we created . . . and destroyed . . . and created again. Here's to you, lads. Raise a glass.

Big up to C.J. O'Connor and Kim Hughes for generously allowing the use of your articles.

The following people also deserve a big, heartfelt thank you. Here they are, in no particular order:

Scotty McClelland, Damyana and Natasha Metez, Fab Claxton, Dan White, Yvonne Matsell, Penny, Maria, Trish Mennell, Sue Weigand, April Benegbi, "Gorilla" Phil Williams, Sue and John Newhouses, Paul MacNeil, Captain Phil Evans, Deana Collins, Richard Cronin,

Kerri Huffman, Tom Richardson, CFNY, Dave Parry, Red Dog Ray (RIP), Fraz, Will McGuirk, Michael Bell, Jacob King, Mike Star, Lisa Borgstadt, Adam Goddard, Janice Both, Brian Sliwinski, Jan Bilek, Vezi Tayyeb, Astrid Fauchon, Adam Brown, Matthew Brown, Phil Butler, Fred Robinson, the Coles, Smalltown Preachers, SKAFACE, Teenage X, Scam Artists, Monday Nuns, Genetic Rhythm, Heebee Gee, the Mindset, Purple Toads, Durango 95, UIC, Voodoo Chicken, the Corndogs, the Wire, Trent Arthur, Torstar, Metroland, Sun Media, the Oshawa Times, and the Durham Chronicle.

Alistair Munro. It all began with you. I think I can speak for Steve when I say, you've been sorely missed. Sleep tight.

Finally, to my absolute favourite person in the whole-wide-world, my uber-cool daughter Zoe. How much love does one man need?

Front cover design—Jacob King

Front cover photo—Lisa Borgstadt

Back cover photo—Trish Mennell

Back cover marketing copy—John Duarte

CHEAT

NITE KLUB

DARE TO DREAM
Written by CLOSS/GOODMAN/GRAHAM/WRIGHT

FANTASY MERRY-GO-ROUND
Written by CLOSS/GOODMAN/GRAHAM/WRIGHT

CITY ASLEEP
Written by CLOSS/GOODMAN/GRAHAM/WRIGHT

COFFEE-MAKER
Written by CLOSS/GOODMAN/GRAHAM/WRIGHT